Moral Algorithms Navigating the Ethics of AI

Understanding the Ethical Landscape in the Age of Artificial Intelligence

Copyright © 2024 by RK Books

All rights reserved.

No part of this publication may be reproduced, distributed, or transmitted in any form or by any means, including photocopying, recording, or other electronic or mechanical methods, without the prior written permission of the publisher, except in the case of brief quotations embodied in critical reviews and certain other noncommercial uses permitted by copyright law.

This book is a work of fiction. Names, characters, places, and incidents are products of the author's imagination or are used fictitiously. Any resemblance to actual events, locales, or persons, living or dead, is entirely coincidental.

Published by |

Table of Contents

Introduction 1
Chapter 1 Ethics in AI 4
    Defining Ethics and its Importance in AI 5
    Historical Context Ethics in Technological Advancements 7
    Ethical Challenges Posed by Artificial Intelligence 10
Chapter 2 Foundations of Artificial Intelligence 14
    Overview of Artificial Intelligence and its Components 15
    Historical Development of Artificial Intelligence 19
    Types of Artificial Intelligence: Narrow vs. General AI 22
Chapter 3 The Evolution of Moral Philosophy 28
    Overview of Moral Philosophy 29
    Major Ethical Theories and their Relevance to AI 34
    Contemporary Approaches to Ethical Decision Making 38
Chapter 4 Ethical Frameworks and Their Application to AI 43
    Utilitarianism and AI Ethics 43
    Deontological Ethics and AI Decision Making 46
    Virtue Ethics in AI Design and Implementation 49
Chapter 5 Bias and Fairness in Algorithmic Decision Making 53
    Understanding Bias in AI Systems 54
    Fairness Metrics and Evaluation Techniques in AI Systems 57
    Addressing Bias and Promoting Fairness in AI Algorithms 61
Chapter 6 Transparency and Accountability in AI Systems 66
    Importance of Transparency in AI Decision Making 66
    Accountability Mechanisms in AI Systems 69

Challenges and Solutions in Ensuring Transparency and Accountability in AI Systems 73

Chapter 7 Privacy and Data Ethics in the Digital Age 78

Privacy Concerns in AI Applications 79

Data Ethics and Responsible Data Use 82

Regulatory Frameworks for Protecting Privacy in AI.............................. 86

Chapter 8 AI and the Future of Work: Implications for Ethics 92

Impact of AI on Employment and Labor Practices 93

Ethical Considerations in AI-driven Workplace Automation.................. 96

Strategies for Ethical AI Adoption in the Workforce 99

Chapter 9 Autonomous Systems and Moral Responsibility 103

Understanding Autonomous Systems and Their Decision Making 104

Moral Agency in AI and Autonomous Agents 108

Assigning Moral Responsibility in Autonomous Systems...................... 112

Chapter 10 Ethical Challenges in Autonomous Vehicles 117

Ethical Dilemmas Faced by Autonomous Vehicles................................ 118

Approaches to Solving Moral Decision Making in Autonomous Vehicle 120

Public Perception and Acceptance of Ethical AI in Transportation....... 125

Introduction

In an era defined by unprecedented technological advancements, the integration of artificial intelligence (AI) into various aspects of our lives has become inevitable. From personalized recommendations on streaming platforms to autonomous vehicles navigating our streets, AI systems are increasingly influencing our decisions and shaping our experiences. However, alongside the promise of innovation and efficiency, the proliferation of AI raises profound ethical questions that demand careful consideration.

This book, "Moral Algorithms: Navigating the Ethics of AI," delves into the intricate intersection of morality and artificial intelligence. In the age of rapidly evolving technology, understanding the ethical landscape surrounding AI is paramount to harnessing its potential while mitigating its risks. As AI systems become more autonomous and pervasive, it becomes imperative to scrutinize the ethical implications of their actions and decisions.

The subtitle of this book, "Understanding the Ethical Landscape in the Age of Artificial Intelligence," encapsulates its core objective: to provide readers with a comprehensive understanding of the ethical challenges posed by AI. By exploring various philosophical frameworks, real-world case studies, and emerging trends, this book aims to equip readers with the knowledge and tools necessary to navigate the complex terrain of moral algorithms.

At the heart of the discussion lies the recognition that AI is not inherently good or bad; rather, its ethical implications are contingent upon how it is designed, deployed, and governed. Thus, a critical examination of the ethical dimensions of AI is essential for fostering responsible innovation and ensuring that AI serves the common good.

The journey begins by laying down the foundations of ethics, exploring diverse moral philosophies that underpin our understanding of right and wrong. From utilitarianism to deontology, each philosophical framework offers valuable insights into how we can evaluate the ethical implications of AI technologies.

Building upon this philosophical groundwork, the book examines the historical development and current landscape of artificial intelligence. By tracing the evolution of AI from its inception to its present-day applications, readers gain a deeper appreciation for the technological advancements that have brought us to the forefront of the AI revolution.

However, as AI continues to advance, so too do the ethical challenges it presents. One such challenge is the issue of bias and fairness in algorithmic decision-making. AI systems, trained on vast datasets reflective of societal biases, have the potential to perpetuate and exacerbate existing inequalities. Thus, ensuring fairness and transparency in AI algorithms is essential for upholding ethical standards and promoting social justice.

Moreover, the rise of autonomous systems raises profound questions about moral responsibility. As machines become increasingly capable of making decisions autonomously, who should be held accountable for their actions? This question lies at the heart of debates surrounding the ethical implications of AI in various domains, from healthcare to criminal justice.

Throughout this book, readers will explore these and other pressing ethical dilemmas, gaining insight into the complexities of moral decision-making in the age of artificial intelligence. By grappling with these issues, we can collectively work towards the development of ethical AI systems that reflect our values and aspirations as a society.

In the chapters that follow, we will embark on a journey through the ethical landscape of AI, navigating the moral algorithms that shape our technological future. It is my hope that this book will serve as a valuable resource for scholars, practitioners, and concerned citizens alike, fostering informed dialogue and responsible action in the pursuit of ethical AI.

Chapter 1
Ethics in AI

Artificial Intelligence (AI) is not just a technological innovation; it is a moral imperative. As AI systems become more pervasive in our society, it's essential to recognize the ethical dimensions inherent in their design, deployment, and impact. In this chapter, we embark on a journey to explore the fundamental principles that underpin the ethical considerations surrounding AI.

Ethics in AI refers to the principles and values that govern the development and use of AI technologies. It encompasses questions of fairness, accountability, transparency, and autonomy. Understanding the ethical implications of AI is crucial because these technologies have the power to shape human behavior, influence societal norms, and redefine our understanding of morality.

Throughout this chapter, we will delve into the foundational concepts of ethics and their relevance to AI. By examining historical precedents, philosophical theories, and real-world examples, we aim to lay the groundwork for a nuanced understanding of the ethical landscape in the age of artificial intelligence. Ultimately, our goal is to equip readers with the tools they need to navigate the complex ethical challenges posed by AI and to foster responsible innovation in this rapidly evolving field.

Defining Ethics and its Importance in AI

Ethics, in its broadest sense, refers to the study of moral principles that govern human behavior and decision-making. It encompasses concepts such as fairness, justice, autonomy, and responsibility. In the context of artificial intelligence (AI), ethics plays a pivotal role in guiding the design, development, and deployment of AI systems. Understanding the ethical implications of AI is essential for ensuring that these technologies align with societal values and contribute to the common good.

At its core, ethics provides a framework for evaluating the impact of AI on individuals, communities, and society as a whole. It prompts us to consider not only the technical capabilities of AI systems but also their broader societal implications. For example, when designing an AI algorithm for predictive policing, ethical considerations might include questions about bias, privacy, and the potential for reinforcing existing social inequalities.

One of the primary reasons why ethics is crucial in AI is the potential for these technologies to shape human behavior and influence societal norms. AI systems are not neutral; they reflect the values and biases of their creators and the data on which they are trained. Without careful consideration of ethical principles, AI systems may perpetuate or exacerbate existing injustices, leading to harmful consequences for marginalized communities.

Moreover, ethics serves as a safeguard against the misuse of AI technologies for nefarious purposes. From autonomous weapons systems to algorithmic discrimination, there are numerous ethical pitfalls associated with AI that must be addressed to prevent harm and ensure accountability. By establishing ethical guidelines and standards for AI development and deployment, we can mitigate these risks and promote the responsible use of these technologies.

Another reason why ethics is essential in AI is its role in fostering trust and confidence in these technologies. As AI becomes increasingly integrated into our daily lives, it is essential for users to have confidence that these systems will act in their best interests and uphold ethical standards. Transparency, accountability, and fairness are essential elements of ethical AI systems that can help build trust and mitigate concerns about privacy, bias, and algorithmic decision-making.

Furthermore, ethics provides a framework for navigating the complex ethical dilemmas that arise in the development and deployment of AI. From questions about the rights of AI systems to concerns about job displacement and economic inequality, there are numerous ethical considerations that must be weighed and balanced to ensure that AI serves the greater good. By engaging in ethical deliberation and dialogue, we can identify potential risks and trade-offs and make informed decisions about how best to harness the power of AI for positive social impact.

In addition to its importance in guiding the development and deployment of AI, ethics also plays a crucial role in shaping public policy and regulation in this area. As AI technologies continue to advance and become more pervasive, policymakers face the challenge of crafting laws and regulations that promote innovation while also protecting individual rights and societal values. Ethical principles provide a foundation for policymakers to develop regulations that strike the right balance between innovation and accountability, ensuring that AI serves the public interest.

Overall, ethics is fundamental to the responsible development and deployment of AI. By considering the ethical implications of these technologies, we can ensure that AI aligns with societal values, promotes fairness and justice, and contributes to the common good. As we continue to explore the potential of AI to transform our world, it is essential to remember that with great power comes great responsibility, and ethics must guide us every step of the way.

Historical Context Ethics in Technological Advancements

Ethics in technological advancements is a subject that spans centuries, reflecting humanity's evolving relationship with innovation, progress, and the ethical implications of new technologies. Throughout history, as societies have developed and embraced new inventions, ethical considerations have arisen, shaping the way these technologies are perceived, regulated, and utilized. In this chapter, we will explore the historical context of ethics in technological advancements, tracing key developments from ancient civilizations to the modern era.

Ancient Civilizations and Ethical Considerations

The history of ethics in technological advancements can be traced back to ancient civilizations such as Mesopotamia, Egypt, and Greece. In these early societies, technological innovations such as agriculture, metallurgy, and writing transformed human life, leading to profound ethical questions about power, governance, and social organization.

For example, in ancient Mesopotamia, the invention of writing by the Sumerians around 3500 BCE revolutionized communication, record-keeping, and administration. However, the dissemination of written laws and edicts raised ethical questions about justice, fairness, and accountability. Who had the authority to write and interpret laws? How were disputes resolved in a literate society? These ethical dilemmas laid the groundwork for the development of legal systems and governance structures that continue to shape our world today.

Similarly, in ancient Greece, the emergence of philosophical schools such as Stoicism and Epicureanism prompted reflection on the ethical implications of technology and progress. Philosophers such as Plato and Aristotle explored questions about the virtuous use of technology, the relationship between humans and nature, and the pursuit of eudaimonia (human flourishing). These philosophical inquiries provided a foundation for ethical reflection on technology that would resonate throughout history.

The Renaissance and the Enlightenment: Humanism and Rationalism

During the Renaissance and the Enlightenment, ethics in technological advancements took on new significance as humanism and rationalism emerged as dominant intellectual currents. The Renaissance saw a resurgence of interest in classical learning, artistic expression, and scientific inquiry, leading to breakthroughs in fields such as anatomy, astronomy, and engineering.

Ethical considerations during this period were closely linked to humanist ideals such as dignity, autonomy, and freedom. Renaissance humanists such as Leonardo da Vinci and Erasmus of Rotterdam celebrated the potential of human creativity and intellect to improve society and enhance human flourishing. However, they also grappled with ethical questions about the responsible use of technology, the role of science in society, and the ethical limits of human knowledge.

The Enlightenment further expanded the scope of ethical reflection on technology, emphasizing reason, empiricism, and progress. Enlightenment thinkers such as Voltaire, Rousseau, and Kant explored questions about the ethical foundations of society, the rights of individuals, and the responsibilities of governments. The emergence of modern science and technology during this period raised new ethical dilemmas about the potential for misuse, exploitation, and harm.

Industrial Revolution: Ethics and Industrialization

The Industrial Revolution marked a pivotal moment in the history of ethics in technological advancements, as rapid industrialization transformed economies, societies, and cultures. The invention of steam power, mechanization, and mass production revolutionized manufacturing, transportation, and communication, leading to unprecedented levels of economic growth and social change.

However, the Industrial Revolution also gave rise to ethical concerns about labor conditions, environmental degradation, and social inequality. As factories proliferated and cities expanded, workers faced harsh working conditions, long hours, and low wages, prompting calls for labor rights, social reforms, and ethical business practices. Ethical philosophers such as Jeremy Bentham and John Stuart Mill advocated for utilitarian principles of greatest good for the greatest number, arguing for policies that would promote the well-being of all members of society.

Moreover, the Industrial Revolution sparked debates about the ethical implications of technological progress and its impact on human dignity, autonomy, and community. Writers such as Mary Shelley, in her novel "Frankenstein," raised questions about the hubris of scientific experimentation and the unintended consequences of technological innovation. These ethical concerns continue to resonate in contemporary debates about the ethical dimensions of emerging technologies such as artificial intelligence, biotechnology, and nanotechnology.

Twentieth Century: Ethics in the Age of Information

The twentieth century witnessed unprecedented advancements in science and technology, from the invention of the airplane and the atomic bomb to the development of computers and the internet. These technological innovations revolutionized every aspect of human life, from communication and transportation to healthcare and warfare.

However, the rapid pace of technological change also raised profound ethical questions about the responsible use of technology, the protection of privacy and civil liberties, and the ethical implications of scientific research. The rise of totalitarian regimes and the atrocities of World War II underscored the need for ethical guidelines and principles to prevent the misuse of technology for destructive purposes.

In response to these challenges, ethical frameworks such as the Nuremberg Code and the Universal Declaration of Human Rights were developed to protect human subjects in scientific experiments and uphold the dignity and rights of individuals. These ethical principles laid the foundation for contemporary debates about the ethical dimensions of emerging technologies such as genetic engineering, artificial intelligence, and biomedicine.

Throughout history, ethics in technological advancements has been a constant theme, reflecting humanity's aspirations, fears, and values. From ancient civilizations to the modern era, ethical considerations have shaped the way we perceive and utilize technology, influencing everything from governance and public policy to individual behavior and social norms. As we navigate the complexities of the twenty-first century, it is essential to draw on the lessons of history to ensure that our technological advancements are guided by ethical principles that promote human flourishing, justice, and sustainability.

Ethical Challenges Posed by Artificial Intelligence

Artificial Intelligence (AI) has emerged as one of the most transformative technologies of the twenty-first century, promising to revolutionize industries, economies, and societies. However, along with its potential benefits, AI also presents a myriad of ethical challenges that must be addressed to ensure that its development and deployment align with societal values, human rights, and ethical principles. In this chapter, we will explore some of the key ethical challenges posed by artificial intelligence and discuss the implications for individuals, communities, and societies at large.

Bias and Fairness

One of the most significant ethical challenges associated with AI is the issue of bias and fairness in algorithmic decision-making. AI systems are trained on vast amounts of data, which can contain inherent biases reflecting historical inequalities and societal prejudices. As a result, AI algorithms may inadvertently perpetuate or exacerbate biases against certain groups, leading to discriminatory outcomes in areas such as hiring, lending, and criminal justice.

Addressing bias in AI requires careful attention to data collection, preprocessing, and algorithm design. It also necessitates transparency and accountability in AI systems to ensure that biases are identified and mitigated. Additionally, there is a need for greater diversity and inclusivity in the development and deployment of AI technologies to minimize the risk of perpetuating existing inequalities.

Privacy and Data Ethics

Another ethical challenge posed by AI is the protection of privacy and the responsible use of data. AI systems rely on vast amounts of personal data to train algorithms and make predictions about individuals' behavior and preferences. However, the indiscriminate collection and use of personal data raise concerns about privacy violations, surveillance, and the erosion of individual autonomy.

To address these concerns, policymakers and industry stakeholders must establish robust data protection regulations and ethical guidelines for the collection, storage, and use of personal data in AI systems. Additionally, individuals should be empowered with greater control over their data and informed consent mechanisms to ensure that their privacy rights are respected in the age of AI.

Transparency and Accountability

Transparency and accountability are essential principles for ensuring the responsible development and deployment of AI technologies. However, AI systems are often complex and opaque, making it challenging for users to understand how decisions are made and hold developers accountable for their actions. Lack of transparency can lead to distrust and skepticism towards AI systems, undermining their adoption and effectiveness.

To promote transparency and accountability in AI, developers should adopt practices such as algorithmic transparency, explainability, and auditability to ensure that AI systems can be scrutinized and understood by users and regulators. Additionally, mechanisms for accountability, such as independent oversight bodies and regulatory frameworks, are needed to hold developers accountable for the ethical implications of their AI technologies.

Autonomy and Human Agency

As AI systems become more sophisticated and autonomous, they raise fundamental questions about human autonomy and agency. There is concern that the increasing reliance on AI for decision-making in areas such as healthcare, transportation, and finance may erode human autonomy and diminish individual agency. Additionally, the deployment of autonomous AI systems in critical domains raises concerns about the delegation of moral responsibility and accountability.

To address these concerns, it is essential to establish clear guidelines and ethical principles for the design and deployment of autonomous AI systems. These principles should prioritize human values and rights, promote human oversight and control, and ensure that AI systems are designed to augment rather than replace human decision-making.

Equity and Access

Finally, AI raises ethical questions about equity and access to technology. While AI has the potential to improve efficiency and productivity, there is a risk that it may exacerbate existing disparities and widen the digital divide between those who have access to AI technologies and those who do not. Additionally, there is concern that AI may be used to further concentrate wealth and power in the hands of a few, exacerbating social inequality and marginalization.

To address these concerns, policymakers and industry stakeholders must prioritize efforts to promote equitable access to AI technologies and ensure that they benefit all members of society, particularly marginalized and vulnerable populations. This may require investments in digital literacy, education, and infrastructure, as well as measures to mitigate the unintended consequences of AI on employment and economic opportunity.

Artificial intelligence presents a host of ethical challenges that must be addressed to ensure that its development and deployment align with societal values and ethical principles. From bias and fairness to privacy and data ethics, transparency and accountability, autonomy and human agency, and equity and access, these challenges underscore the need for thoughtful deliberation, regulation, and ethical leadership in the age of AI. By addressing these challenges proactively, we can harness the transformative potential of AI while minimizing its risks and maximizing its benefits for individuals, communities, and societies worldwide.

Chapter 2
Foundations of Artificial Intelligence

Artificial Intelligence (AI) stands at the forefront of modern technological innovation, promising to revolutionize industries, reshape economies, and redefine the human experience. At its core, AI seeks to replicate and enhance human-like intelligence in machines, enabling them to perceive, reason, and act autonomously in complex environments. In this chapter, we delve into the foundational principles that underpin the field of artificial intelligence, tracing its historical development, exploring its fundamental concepts, and examining its diverse applications.

From its origins in the early days of computer science to its contemporary manifestations in machine learning and neural networks, the field of artificial intelligence has undergone a remarkable evolution. Through a combination of mathematical theory, computational algorithms, and empirical experimentation, researchers have made significant strides in advancing our understanding of intelligence and creating machines capable of exhibiting intelligent behavior.

In this chapter, we will explore the key components of artificial intelligence, including problem-solving techniques, knowledge representation, and learning algorithms. We will examine the philosophical underpinnings of AI, considering questions about the nature of intelligence, consciousness, and creativity. Additionally, we will explore the practical applications of AI across a wide range of domains, from robotics and autonomous vehicles to natural language processing and healthcare.

By understanding the foundations of artificial intelligence, we gain insight into the capabilities and limitations of AI systems and the ethical considerations that accompany their development and deployment. As we embark on this exploration, we are reminded of the immense potential of AI to transform our world and the responsibility we bear to ensure that its impact is aligned with our values and aspirations.

Overview of Artificial Intelligence and its Components

Artificial Intelligence (AI) is a branch of computer science that aims to create intelligent machines capable of performing tasks that typically require human intelligence. These tasks include problem-solving, learning, reasoning, perception, language understanding, and decision-making. AI systems can be broadly classified into two categories: Narrow AI, also known as Weak AI, and General AI, also known as Strong AI.

Narrow AI:

Narrow AI refers to AI systems that are designed and trained for specific tasks or domains. These systems excel at performing well-defined tasks within a limited context but lack the general intelligence and adaptability of humans. Examples of narrow AI applications include speech recognition, image classification, recommendation systems, and autonomous vehicles.

General AI:

General AI, on the other hand, refers to AI systems that possess the ability to understand, learn, and apply knowledge across a wide range of domains, similar to human intelligence. General AI systems have the potential to perform any intellectual task that a human can, including reasoning, problem-solving, creativity, and social interaction. However, achieving true general intelligence remains a significant challenge in the field of AI, and researchers continue to explore ways to develop AI systems that can exhibit human-like intelligence.

Components of Artificial Intelligence:

Artificial Intelligence encompasses a variety of components, techniques, and methodologies that enable machines to exhibit intelligent behavior. Some of the key components of AI include:

Machine Learning: Machine learning is a subfield of AI that focuses on developing algorithms and techniques that enable machines to learn from data and improve their performance over time without being explicitly programmed. Machine learning algorithms can be categorized into supervised learning, unsupervised learning, and reinforcement learning, each of which has its own set of techniques and applications.

Natural Language Processing (NLP): Natural language processing is a subfield of AI that focuses on enabling computers to understand, interpret, and generate human language. NLP techniques are used in applications such as speech recognition, language translation, sentiment analysis, and chatbots.

Computer Vision: Computer vision is a subfield of AI that focuses on enabling computers to interpret and understand visual information from the real world. Computer vision techniques are used in applications such as image recognition, object detection, facial recognition, and medical imaging.

Knowledge Representation and Reasoning: Knowledge representation and reasoning is a subfield of AI that focuses on developing formalisms and techniques for representing and reasoning about knowledge in AI systems. These techniques enable AI systems to encode and manipulate knowledge in a way that supports intelligent behavior and decision-making.

Robotics: Robotics is a subfield of AI that focuses on developing autonomous machines that can perceive, reason, and act in the physical world. Robotics techniques are used in applications such as industrial automation, autonomous vehicles, drones, and healthcare robotics.

Expert Systems: Expert systems are AI systems that are designed to mimic the decision-making abilities of human experts in specific domains. These systems use knowledge representation, inference engines, and reasoning algorithms to emulate the decision-making process of human experts and provide recommendations or solutions to complex problems.

Neural Networks: Neural networks are a class of AI algorithms that are inspired by the structure and function of the human brain. These algorithms consist of interconnected nodes, or neurons, that process and transmit information using mathematical functions. Neural networks are used in applications such as deep learning, pattern recognition, and predictive modeling.

Applications of Artificial Intelligence:

Artificial Intelligence has a wide range of applications across various industries and domains. Some of the key applications of AI include:

Healthcare: AI is being used in healthcare for tasks such as medical diagnosis, personalized treatment planning, drug discovery, and patient monitoring.

Finance: AI is being used in finance for tasks such as fraud detection, risk assessment, algorithmic trading, and customer service.

Transportation: AI is being used in transportation for tasks such as autonomous vehicles, traffic management, route optimization, and predictive maintenance.

Retail: AI is being used in retail for tasks such as demand forecasting, personalized marketing, inventory management, and customer service.

Manufacturing: AI is being used in manufacturing for tasks such as predictive maintenance, quality control, supply chain optimization, and robotic automation.

Customer Service: AI is being used in customer service for tasks such as chatbots, virtual assistants, sentiment analysis, and customer relationship management.

Ethical Considerations in Artificial Intelligence:

While AI holds tremendous potential to benefit society, it also raises ethical concerns and challenges that must be addressed. Some of the key ethical considerations in AI include:

Bias and Fairness: AI systems can exhibit bias and discrimination due to the biases present in training data or the algorithms themselves. Ensuring fairness and equity in AI systems is essential to prevent harm and promote social justice.

Privacy and Security: AI systems often rely on large amounts of personal data, raising concerns about privacy violations and data breaches. Protecting individuals' privacy and ensuring the security of their data are critical ethical considerations in AI.

Transparency and Accountability: AI systems can be opaque and difficult to understand, making it challenging to assess their decisions and hold developers accountable for their actions. Promoting transparency and accountability in AI systems is essential to build trust and mitigate risks.

Autonomy and Agency: AI systems have the potential to impact human autonomy and agency, leading to concerns about control, accountability, and responsibility. Ensuring that humans retain control over AI systems and are empowered to make informed decisions is essential to protect individual autonomy and agency.

Equity and Access: AI has the potential to exacerbate existing disparities and widen the digital divide, leading to concerns about equity and access. Ensuring equitable access to AI technologies and addressing the needs of marginalized and vulnerable populations are critical ethical considerations in AI.

Artificial Intelligence is a rapidly evolving field with significant implications for society, economy, and culture. By understanding the components of AI, its applications, and the ethical considerations it raises, we can harness its potential to address some of the most pressing challenges facing humanity while mitigating its risks and ensuring that it serves the common good. Continued research, innovation, and ethical reflection are essential to navigate the complex landscape of Artificial Intelligence responsibly.

Historical Development of Artificial Intelligence

The history of Artificial Intelligence (AI) is a fascinating journey that spans centuries, marked by significant milestones, breakthroughs, and setbacks. The quest to create intelligent machines that can emulate human-like behavior and cognition has captivated the minds of scientists, philosophers, and inventors throughout history. In this chapter, we will explore the historical development of AI, tracing its origins from ancient civilizations to the modern era of deep learning and neural networks.

Ancient Beginnings:

The roots of AI can be traced back to ancient civilizations, where myths, legends, and philosophical inquiries laid the groundwork for the concept of artificial beings with human-like qualities. In ancient Greek mythology, tales of mechanical servants, such as Talos, the bronze automaton, and Hephaestus' automated workshop, foreshadowed humanity's fascination with creating artificial life.

The Renaissance and Early Modern Era:

During the Renaissance and Early Modern Era, advancements in mathematics, science, and philosophy laid the foundation for modern AI. Renaissance thinkers such as Leonardo da Vinci explored the concept of artificial beings in his sketches of humanoid robots and mechanical knights. Similarly, the philosopher René Descartes speculated about the possibility of creating artificial animals and humans in his work "Discourse on the Method."

The Birth of Computing:

The birth of modern computing in the mid-20th century marked a significant milestone in the development of AI. In the 1940s and 1950s, pioneers such as Alan Turing, John von Neumann, and Claude Shannon laid the theoretical foundations of computer science and information theory. Turing's seminal paper "Computing Machinery and Intelligence" proposed the famous Turing Test as a criterion for determining a machine's intelligence.

Early AI Research:

The term "Artificial Intelligence" was coined in 1956 during the Dartmouth Summer Research Project on Artificial Intelligence, where scientists and researchers gathered to explore the possibilities of creating machines that could exhibit intelligent behavior. The participants, including John McCarthy, Marvin Minsky, Herbert Simon, and Allen Newell, laid the groundwork for AI as an interdisciplinary field encompassing computer science, cognitive psychology, and logic.

Symbolic AI and Expert Systems:

In the 1960s and 1970s, researchers focused on symbolic AI, also known as "Good Old-Fashioned AI" (GOFAI), which used symbolic logic and rule-based systems to emulate human reasoning and problem-solving. This approach led to the development of expert systems, AI programs that could mimic the knowledge and decision-making abilities of human experts in specific domains. Expert systems found applications in fields such as medicine, finance, and engineering.

The AI Winter:

Despite early optimism and enthusiasm, the field of AI faced setbacks and challenges in the 1970s and 1980s, leading to a period known as the "AI Winter." Funding cuts, unrealistic expectations, and a lack of progress in solving complex AI problems led to a decline in interest and investment in AI research. Many AI projects were abandoned, and the field fell out of favor with the public and policymakers.

The Rise of Neural Networks:

In the 1980s and 1990s, researchers began to explore alternative approaches to AI, including neural networks, which were inspired by the structure and function of the human brain. Neural networks, also known as connectionist models, showed promise in solving pattern recognition and classification tasks and led to significant advancements in machine learning and AI.

Machine Learning and Data-Driven AI:

The 21st century witnessed a resurgence of interest and investment in AI, fueled by advancements in machine learning, big data, and computational power. Researchers developed powerful algorithms and techniques, such as deep learning, reinforcement learning, and unsupervised learning, that enabled machines to learn from vast amounts of data and make predictions with unprecedented accuracy.

Contemporary AI Applications:

Today, AI is ubiquitous in our daily lives, powering a wide range of applications and technologies. From virtual assistants and recommendation systems to autonomous vehicles and healthcare diagnostics, AI is revolutionizing industries, transforming economies, and reshaping society. However, with the rise of AI comes a new set of challenges and ethical considerations, including concerns about bias, transparency, privacy, and the impact of automation on jobs and inequality.

The Future of AI:

As AI continues to advance, researchers are exploring new frontiers in artificial intelligence, including quantum computing, brain-computer interfaces, and artificial general intelligence (AGI). AGI, also known as human-level AI, is the ultimate goal of AI research, aiming to create machines that possess the same level of intelligence and cognitive abilities as humans. While AGI remains a distant prospect, the pursuit of artificial intelligence continues to captivate the imagination and drive innovation in the 21st century.

The historical development of AI is a testament to humanity's enduring quest to understand intelligence and create intelligent machines. From ancient myths and philosophical inquiries to modern computing and machine learning, the journey of AI is a story of curiosity, ingenuity, and perseverance. As we look to the future, the possibilities of AI are boundless, offering both opportunities and challenges that will shape the course of human civilization for generations to come.

Types of Artificial Intelligence: Narrow vs. General AI

Artificial Intelligence (AI) is a broad field that encompasses a variety of approaches, techniques, and applications aimed at creating machines capable of intelligent behavior. Within the realm of AI, two primary categories are often distinguished: Narrow AI, also known as Weak AI, and General AI, also known as Strong AI. In this chapter, we will explore these two types of AI, their characteristics, capabilities, and implications for society.

Narrow AI:

Narrow AI refers to AI systems that are designed and trained for specific tasks or domains. These systems excel at performing well-defined tasks within a limited context but lack the general intelligence and adaptability of humans. Narrow AI is the most prevalent form of AI in use today and encompasses a wide range of applications across various industries and domains.

Characteristics of Narrow AI:

Specificity: Narrow AI systems are tailored to perform specific tasks or solve specific problems within a well-defined domain. These tasks may include speech recognition, image classification, natural language processing, recommendation systems, and autonomous driving, among others.

Limited Context: Narrow AI systems operate within a limited context or domain and may struggle to generalize their knowledge and skills to new or unfamiliar situations. For example, a speech recognition system trained on English may not perform well when presented with speech in another language.

Task-Oriented: Narrow AI systems are task-oriented and optimized for efficiency and performance in completing specific tasks. They are typically trained on large datasets using supervised or reinforcement learning techniques to optimize their performance on a particular task.

Narrow Expertise: Narrow AI systems exhibit expertise in their specific domain but lack the broader knowledge and cognitive abilities of humans. They excel at narrow, specialized tasks but may struggle with tasks that require general intelligence, creativity, or common sense reasoning.

Examples of Narrow AI:

Virtual Assistants: Virtual assistants such as Siri, Alexa, and Google Assistant are examples of narrow AI systems that are designed to perform specific tasks such as answering questions, setting reminders, and providing information based on user queries.

Image Recognition: Image recognition systems used in applications such as facial recognition, object detection, and medical imaging are examples of narrow AI systems trained to recognize patterns and classify images within specific domains.

Recommendation Systems: Recommendation systems used in e-commerce platforms, streaming services, and social media platforms are examples of narrow AI systems that analyze user behavior and preferences to recommend products, content, or connections tailored to individual users.

Autonomous Vehicles: Autonomous vehicles, such as self-driving cars, drones, and robots, are examples of narrow AI systems designed to navigate and operate within specific environments, such as roads, airspace, or warehouses, using sensors, cameras, and algorithms.

General AI:

General AI, on the other hand, refers to AI systems that possess the ability to understand, learn, and apply knowledge across a wide range of domains, similar to human intelligence. General AI represents the ultimate goal of AI research and is characterized by its capacity for reasoning, problem-solving, creativity, and adaptability.

Characteristics of General AI:

Versatility: General AI systems exhibit versatility and adaptability in performing a wide range of tasks across multiple domains. Unlike narrow AI systems, which are specialized for specific tasks, general AI systems can transfer their knowledge and skills to new or unfamiliar situations.

Contextual Understanding: General AI systems possess a deep understanding of context and can interpret and respond to complex situations in a manner that is contextually appropriate. They can reason about uncertain or ambiguous information, make judgments based on incomplete data, and adapt their behavior to changing circumstances.

Learning Abilities: General AI systems have the ability to learn from experience, acquire new knowledge, and improve their performance over time. They can engage in lifelong learning, explore new domains, and refine their understanding through observation, experimentation, and feedback.

Human-Like Intelligence: General AI systems exhibit human-like intelligence and cognitive abilities, including reasoning, problem-solving, creativity, and social interaction. They can engage in complex tasks that require abstract thinking, intuition, and common sense reasoning, such as planning, decision-making, and language understanding.

Challenges of General AI:

Achieving General AI remains a significant challenge in the field of AI research due to several technical, ethical, and philosophical hurdles. Some of the key challenges of General AI include:

Computational Complexity: General AI requires sophisticated algorithms, massive computational resources, and vast amounts of data to simulate the complexity of human intelligence. Developing

AI systems capable of generalizing across diverse domains and contexts poses significant computational challenges.

Ethical Considerations: General AI raises ethical concerns and dilemmas regarding autonomy, accountability, privacy, and the impact of AI on society. Ensuring that General AI systems adhere to ethical principles, respect human rights, and serve the common good is essential to mitigate potential risks and harms.

Safety and Control: General AI systems have the potential to surpass human intelligence and capabilities, raising concerns about control, safety, and unintended consequences. Ensuring that General AI systems are aligned with human values, goals, and priorities is essential to prevent undesirable outcomes and ensure their safe and beneficial deployment.

Existential Risks: Some researchers and experts have raised concerns about the existential risks associated with General AI, such as the potential for AI systems to surpass human intelligence and pose an existential threat to humanity. Addressing these risks requires careful consideration of the long-term implications of AI development and deployment.

Narrow AI and General AI represent two distinct approaches to artificial intelligence, each with its own characteristics, capabilities, and implications. Narrow AI excels at performing specific tasks within well-defined domains and is prevalent in a wide range of applications across various industries and domains. General AI, on the other hand, possesses the ability to understand, learn, and apply knowledge across a wide range of domains, similar to human intelligence, but remains a distant prospect in AI research.

As we continue to advance the field of AI, it is essential to recognize the strengths and limitations of both Narrow AI and General AI and consider the ethical, social, and philosophical implications of their development and deployment. By understanding the types of AI and their respective challenges and opportunities, we can harness the transformative potential of AI while ensuring that it serves the common good and aligns with human values and aspirations.

Chapter 3
The Evolution of Moral Philosophy

Moral philosophy, also known as ethics, is a discipline that has been central to human inquiry since antiquity. It explores fundamental questions about what is right and wrong, good and bad, and how individuals and societies should behave. The evolution of moral philosophy reflects humanity's quest to understand the nature of morality, the foundations of ethical principles, and the implications for human conduct and social organization.

In this chapter, we will embark on a journey through the history of moral philosophy, tracing its development from ancient civilizations to the modern era. We will explore the insights of prominent philosophers, religious thinkers, and moral theorists who have shaped our understanding of morality and ethics. From the ethical teachings of Confucius and Aristotle to the moral theories of Kant and Mill, we will examine the diverse perspectives and approaches that have emerged throughout history.

By exploring the evolution of moral philosophy, we gain insight into the timeless questions and perennial dilemmas that have preoccupied human beings for millennia. We also come to appreciate the richness and complexity of moral thought and the ongoing quest to cultivate virtue, promote justice, and live ethically meaningful lives. As we navigate the landscape of moral philosophy, we are reminded of the enduring significance of ethics in shaping human values, actions, and aspirations.

Overview of Moral Philosophy

Moral philosophy, also known as ethics, is a branch of philosophy that explores questions about what is right and wrong, good and bad, and how individuals and societies should behave. It seeks to understand the nature of morality, the foundations of ethical principles, and the implications for human conduct and social organization. Moral philosophy is a timeless and universal endeavor that has been central to human inquiry since antiquity, shaping the way we think about ethics, justice, and the good life.

Foundations of Moral Philosophy:

The foundations of moral philosophy lie in the human capacity for moral reasoning, reflection, and deliberation. From ancient civilizations to modern societies, human beings have grappled with questions about morality and ethics, seeking to understand the principles that guide virtuous behavior and the reasons for adhering to moral norms. While moral beliefs and practices may vary across cultures and traditions, moral philosophy seeks to uncover universal principles and values that transcend cultural differences and provide a basis for ethical inquiry.

Key Concepts in Moral Philosophy:

Moral philosophy encompasses a variety of key concepts and theories that provide frameworks for understanding morality and ethical decision-making. Some of the fundamental concepts in moral philosophy include:

Moral Agency: Moral agency refers to the capacity of individuals to act autonomously and make morally significant choices. Moral agents are responsible for their actions and accountable for the consequences of their decisions, reflecting their capacity for moral judgment, deliberation, and choice.

Moral Values: Moral values are principles or standards that guide ethical behavior and judgments about what is right and wrong. These values may include concepts such as honesty, integrity, fairness, compassion, and respect for others, which serve as the foundation for moral reasoning and action.

Moral Obligation: Moral obligation refers to the duty or responsibility individuals have to act in accordance with moral principles and norms. Moral obligations may arise from various sources, including religious beliefs, social norms, philosophical theories, and personal conscience, and may impose duties to refrain from harm, promote the common good, or uphold justice and fairness.

Ethical Theories: Ethical theories are systematic frameworks for evaluating moral dilemmas and making ethical judgments. These theories provide principles, criteria, and methods for determining what actions are morally right or wrong, including consequentialist theories such as utilitarianism, deontological theories such as Kantian ethics, and virtue ethics, which focus on the cultivation of virtuous character traits.

Historical Development of Moral Philosophy:

The history of moral philosophy is a rich and diverse tapestry that spans centuries, reflecting the insights, debates, and contributions of philosophers, theologians, and thinkers from various traditions and cultures. From ancient Greece and China to medieval Europe and the modern era, moral philosophy has evolved in response to changing intellectual, social, and cultural contexts, shaping the way we understand and engage with ethical questions.

Ancient Moral Philosophy:

Ancient civilizations such as Greece, China, India, and the Middle East laid the foundations for moral philosophy, exploring questions about virtue, justice, and the good life. In ancient Greece, philosophers such as Socrates, Plato, and Aristotle sought to understand the nature of virtue and the role of reason in moral decision-making. Aristotle's Nicomachean Ethics, for example, explores the concept of eudaimonia, or human flourishing, and the virtues that lead to a well-lived life.

In ancient China, Confucianism emphasized the importance of moral cultivation, social harmony, and filial piety, advocating for the practice of benevolence, righteousness, and propriety in interpersonal relationships. Confucian ethics focused on the cultivation of moral virtues such as ren (benevolence), li (ritual propriety), and xiao (filial piety) as the foundation for a harmonious society.

Medieval and Renaissance Moral Philosophy:

During the medieval and Renaissance periods, moral philosophy was influenced by religious traditions, theological debates, and philosophical inquiries. Christian theologians such as Augustine and Aquinas drew on the teachings of the Bible and the writings of Greek and Roman philosophers to develop ethical theories grounded in faith, reason, and natural law.

Augustine's concept of the "City of God" contrasted with the "City of Man" emphasized the tension between divine and earthly values, while Aquinas's synthesis of Christian theology and Aristotelian philosophy sought to reconcile faith and reason in the pursuit of moral truth.

In the Renaissance, humanist philosophers such as Erasmus and Montaigne emphasized the importance of individual conscience, human dignity, and moral autonomy, challenging traditional religious and political authorities and advocating for the cultivation of personal virtue and moral integrity.

Modern Moral Philosophy:

The Enlightenment marked a pivotal moment in the development of modern moral philosophy, as philosophers such as Immanuel Kant, Jeremy Bentham, and John Stuart Mill sought to ground ethics in reason, autonomy, and utility. Kant's deontological ethics emphasized the moral worth of rational beings and the importance of moral duties derived from the categorical imperative, while Bentham and Mill's utilitarianism focused on maximizing happiness and minimizing suffering as the basis for ethical decision-making.

In the 20th century, moral philosophy witnessed a resurgence of interest in virtue ethics, as philosophers such as Alasdair MacIntyre and Martha Nussbaum sought to revive Aristotelian ethics and explore the role of character, virtue, and narrative in moral life. Contemporary moral philosophy continues to grapple with pressing ethical questions, including issues such as global justice, environmental ethics, and the ethics of emerging technologies.

Contemporary Debates in Moral Philosophy:

Contemporary moral philosophy is characterized by ongoing debates and discussions about a wide range of ethical issues and dilemmas. These debates often center on questions about the nature of moral value, the justification of ethical principles, and the application of moral theories to real-world problems. Some of the key debates in contemporary moral philosophy include:

Metaethics vs Normative Ethics: Metaethics explores the nature of moral judgments and the foundations of ethical principles, asking questions about the objectivity of moral values, the meaning of moral language, and the existence of moral truths. Normative ethics, on the other hand, focuses on the content of moral principles and the criteria for determining what actions are morally right or wrong, including consequentialist, deontological, and virtue ethical theories.

Ethics and Religion: The relationship between ethics and religion is a perennial topic of debate in moral philosophy, with some philosophers arguing that moral principles are grounded in religious beliefs or divine commandments, while others maintain that ethics can be based on secular principles such as reason, empathy, and human flourishing.

Ethics and Politics: The intersection of ethics and politics raises questions about the role of government, law, and social institutions in promoting justice, equality, and the common good. Debates about distributive justice, human rights, and the ethics of citizenship highlight the tensions between individual freedoms and collective responsibilities in society.

Applied Ethics: Applied ethics examines ethical issues and dilemmas in specific domains, such as bioethics, environmental ethics, business ethics, and technology ethics. These fields explore questions about the ethical implications of scientific advances, technological innovations, and social practices, and seek to develop ethical guidelines and frameworks for addressing ethical challenges in these areas.

Moral philosophy is a dynamic and interdisciplinary field that continues to evolve in response to changing intellectual, social, and cultural contexts. From ancient civilizations to modern societies, human beings have grappled with questions about morality and ethics, seeking to understand the nature of right and wrong and the principles that guide virtuous behavior. By exploring the foundations, historical development, and contemporary debates in moral philosophy, we gain insight into the complexities of ethical reasoning and the enduring quest for moral truth and wisdom. As we navigate the landscape of moral philosophy, we are reminded of the importance of ethical reflection, dialogue, and engagement in shaping a more just, compassionate, and flourishing world.

Major Ethical Theories and their Relevance to AI

Ethical theories provide frameworks for evaluating moral dilemmas and making ethical judgments about right and wrong conduct. These theories offer different perspectives on the nature of morality, the principles that guide ethical behavior, and the criteria for determining what actions are morally permissible or obligatory. In the context of Artificial Intelligence (AI), ethical theories play a crucial role in addressing ethical challenges and guiding the development, deployment, and use of AI systems. In this chapter, we will explore some of the major ethical theories and their relevance to AI, examining how they inform ethical considerations in AI research, design, and implementation.

Utilitarianism:

Utilitarianism is a consequentialist ethical theory that evaluates the morality of actions based on their outcomes or consequences. According to utilitarianism, the right action is the one that maximizes overall happiness or utility and minimizes suffering or harm for the greatest number of individuals. Utilitarianism focuses on the principle of utility, which holds that actions are morally right if they produce the greatest amount of happiness or pleasure and minimize the greatest amount of pain or suffering.

Relevance to AI:

Utilitarianism provides a framework for evaluating the ethical implications of AI systems based on their impact on human welfare and well-being. In the context of AI, utilitarian considerations may involve assessing the potential benefits and harms of AI applications, such as autonomous vehicles, healthcare diagnostics, and predictive analytics. Utilitarianism can inform decisions about the design, deployment, and regulation of AI systems to maximize overall social welfare and minimize negative consequences for individuals and communities.

Deontological Ethics:

Deontological ethics, often associated with the moral philosophy of Immanuel Kant, emphasizes the importance of moral duties, principles, and rules in guiding ethical behavior. According to deontological ethics, certain actions are inherently right or wrong, regardless of their consequences, based on principles of duty, rights, and respect for persons. Deontological theories posit that individuals have moral obligations to act in accordance with universalizable rules or principles, such as the categorical imperative, which requires treating others as ends in themselves rather than as means to an end.

Relevance to AI:

Deontological ethics provides a framework for evaluating the ethical implications of AI systems based on principles of autonomy, dignity, and respect for human rights. In the context of AI, deontological considerations may involve ensuring that AI systems respect individual autonomy, privacy, and dignity, and adhere to ethical principles such as informed consent, fairness, and transparency. Deontological ethics can inform decisions about the design, implementation, and governance of AI systems to ensure that they uphold fundamental moral principles and protect the rights and interests of individuals.

Virtue Ethics:

Virtue ethics, rooted in the moral philosophy of Aristotle and other ancient thinkers, emphasizes the cultivation of virtuous character traits and the pursuit of eudaimonia, or human flourishing. According to virtue ethics, ethical behavior arises from the development of virtuous habits, dispositions, and qualities of character, such as courage, honesty, compassion, and wisdom. Virtue ethics focuses on the moral agent rather than the actions themselves, emphasizing the importance of moral education, self-reflection, and the cultivation of moral excellence.

Relevance to AI:

Virtue ethics provides a framework for evaluating the ethical implications of AI systems based on the character and intentions of the individuals involved in their development, deployment, and use. In the context of AI, virtue ethical considerations may involve promoting virtues such as honesty, integrity, empathy, and accountability among AI researchers, engineers, and policymakers. Virtue ethics can inform decisions about the ethical design, implementation, and governance of AI systems by emphasizing the importance of ethical character and moral integrity in all aspects of AI development and deployment.

Contractualism:

Contractualism is a moral theory that emphasizes the importance of social agreements, contracts, and mutual agreements in determining the moral principles and rules that govern human behavior. According to contractualism, moral principles are derived from the hypothetical consent of rational agents who agree to abide by certain rules or norms that promote mutual benefit and cooperation. Contractualist theories posit that moral rules are justified if they can be endorsed by all rational agents under fair and equal conditions.

Relevance to AI:

Contractualism provides a framework for evaluating the ethical implications of AI systems based on principles of fairness, reciprocity, and mutual agreement. In the context of AI, contractualist considerations may involve ensuring that AI systems respect the rights and interests of all stakeholders, including users, communities, and society as a whole. Contractualism can inform decisions about the design, deployment, and regulation of AI systems by promoting principles of fairness, transparency, and accountability that are acceptable to all parties involved.

Feminist Ethics:

Feminist ethics is a moral theory that emphasizes the importance of gender equality, social justice, and the experiences of women in moral reasoning and decision-making. Feminist ethics critiques traditional ethical theories for their emphasis on abstract principles, impartiality, and universality, arguing for an ethics that is grounded in concrete social contexts, relationships, and experiences. Feminist ethics seeks to address issues of power, oppression, and discrimination in moral philosophy and promote the values of care, empathy, and solidarity.

Relevance to AI:

Feminist ethics provides a framework for evaluating the ethical implications of AI systems based on principles of gender equality, social justice, and inclusivity. In the context of AI, feminist ethical considerations may involve addressing issues of bias, discrimination, and inequality in AI algorithms, datasets, and decision-making processes. Feminist ethics can inform decisions about the design, deployment, and regulation of AI systems by promoting diversity, inclusion, and social justice in AI research, development, and implementation.

Ethical theories play a crucial role in guiding ethical considerations in AI research, design, and implementation. By drawing on principles of utilitarianism, deontological ethics, virtue ethics, contractualism, feminist ethics, and other moral theories, we can assess the ethical implications of AI systems and make informed decisions about their development, deployment, and use. By integrating ethical principles into AI research and practice, we can ensure that AI technologies contribute to the well-being and flourishing of individuals and communities, while respecting their rights, dignity, and autonomy. As AI continues to advance and proliferate in society, ethical theories provide valuable frameworks for addressing the complex ethical challenges and dilemmas that arise in the age of artificial intelligence.

Contemporary Approaches to Ethical Decision Making

Ethical decision making is a complex process that involves weighing competing interests, values, and principles to determine the morally right course of action. In contemporary ethics, various approaches have been developed to guide individuals and organizations in making ethical decisions in diverse contexts. These approaches draw on ethical theories, principles, frameworks, and methodologies to analyze ethical dilemmas, evaluate options, and justify moral judgments

1. Ethical Decision Making Models:

Ethical decision making models provide structured frameworks for analyzing ethical dilemmas and guiding individuals through the process of making morally sound decisions. These models typically involve a series of steps or stages that help identify relevant factors, clarify values and goals, consider alternative courses of action, and assess the potential consequences of each option. Some of the most widely used ethical decision making models include:

a) The Ethical Decision Making Process:

This model, proposed by Rest et al. (1986), outlines a six-step process for ethical decision making:

1. **Identify the problem:** Define the ethical issue or dilemma and identify the stakeholders involved.

2. **Gather information:** Collect relevant facts, information, and perspectives to understand the context and implications of the ethical dilemma.

3. **Identify relevant ethical principles:** Consider relevant ethical theories, principles, and values that may apply to the situation.

4. **Generate alternative courses of action:** Brainstorm and evaluate different options for resolving the ethical dilemma.

5. **Evaluate alternatives:** Assess the potential consequences, risks, and benefits of each alternative and consider the principles and values at stake.

6. **Make a decision:** Choose the course of action that best aligns with ethical principles, values, and goals.

b) The Four-Component Model of Ethical Decision Making:

This model, proposed by Trevino et al. (2006), emphasizes four components of ethical decision making:

1. **Moral awareness:** Recognize that an ethical issue or dilemma exists and understand its significance.

2. **Moral judgment:** Analyze the ethical dimensions of the situation and determine the right course of action.

3. **Moral intent:** Formulate a commitment to act in accordance with ethical principles and values.

4. **Ethical behavior:** Follow through on the decision and implement the chosen course of action in practice.

2. Ethical Frameworks and Principles:

Ethical frameworks and principles provide guiding principles and standards for ethical decision making, drawing on moral theories, values, and norms to evaluate actions and outcomes. These frameworks help individuals and organizations identify ethical considerations, assess the moral implications of decisions, and justify their choices based on ethical principles. Some of the key ethical frameworks and principles include:

a) Consequentialism:

Consequentialist frameworks evaluate the morality of actions based on their outcomes or consequences, focusing on maximizing overall happiness, well-being, or utility. Utilitarianism, for example, is a consequentialist theory that holds that the right action is the one that produces the greatest amount of happiness or pleasure and minimizes suffering or harm for the greatest number of individuals.

b) Deontology:

Deontological frameworks emphasize the importance of moral duties, principles, and rules in guiding ethical behavior, regardless of the consequences. Deontological theories, such as Kantian ethics, posit that certain actions are inherently right or wrong based on principles of duty, rights, and respect for persons, and individuals have moral obligations to act in accordance with universalizable rules or principles.

c) Virtue Ethics:

Virtue ethics focuses on the character, virtues, and moral excellence of individuals, emphasizing the cultivation of virtuous character traits such as courage, honesty, compassion, and wisdom. Virtue ethical frameworks evaluate actions based on the character and intentions of the moral agent rather than the consequences, emphasizing the importance of moral education, self-reflection, and the development of virtuous habits.

d) Principlism:

Principlism is an ethical approach that identifies a set of fundamental moral principles or values that serve as the basis for ethical decision making. The four principles of biomedical ethics —

autonomy, beneficence, nonmaleficence, and justice—form the core of principlist frameworks and are applied to analyze ethical dilemmas and justify moral judgments in healthcare and related fields.

3. Applied Ethical Analysis:

Applied ethical analysis involves applying ethical theories, principles, and frameworks to analyze specific ethical issues, dilemmas, or cases in real-world contexts. This approach focuses on identifying ethical considerations, evaluating competing values and interests, and proposing ethically justified solutions or recommendations. Applied ethical analysis may involve:

a) Case Studies:

Case studies provide concrete examples of ethical dilemmas or dilemmas in specific contexts, such as healthcare, business, technology, or environmental ethics. Case studies present ethical dilemmas, scenarios, or dilemmas and prompt individuals to analyze the ethical dimensions of the situation, consider relevant ethical theories and principles, and propose solutions or recommendations based on ethical considerations.

b) Ethical Impact Assessments:

Ethical impact assessments are tools or methodologies used to evaluate the ethical implications of policies, practices, technologies, or decisions before they are implemented. Ethical impact assessments involve identifying potential ethical risks, harms, and benefits, assessing the moral dimensions of the situation, and developing strategies to mitigate ethical concerns and promote ethical outcomes.

c) Ethical Codes and Guidelines:

Ethical codes, guidelines, and standards provide norms, principles, and rules that govern professional conduct and behavior in specific domains or professions. These codes and guidelines help individuals and organizations navigate ethical dilemmas, uphold ethical standards, and promote ethical behavior in their respective fields. Ethical codes and guidelines may be developed by professional associations, regulatory bodies, or industry organizations and are intended to guide ethical decision making and conduct in practice.

Contemporary approaches to ethical decision making provide valuable frameworks, principles, and methodologies for analyzing ethical dilemmas, evaluating options, and justifying moral judgments in diverse contexts. By drawing on ethical theories, frameworks, and applied ethical analysis, individuals and organizations can navigate complex ethical challenges, promote ethical values and principles, and make informed decisions that uphold moral integrity and promote the common good. As ethical decision making continues to evolve in response to changing social, cultural, and technological dynamics, these approaches offer valuable tools and resources for addressing ethical dilemmas and promoting ethical behavior in society.

Chapter 4
Ethical Frameworks and Their Application to AI

In the rapidly evolving landscape of Artificial Intelligence (AI), ethical considerations play a pivotal role in shaping the development, deployment, and impact of AI technologies. Ethical frameworks provide structured approaches for analyzing the ethical implications of AI systems, guiding researchers, developers, policymakers, and stakeholders in navigating complex ethical dilemmas and making morally informed decisions. In this chapter, we will explore various ethical frameworks and their application to AI, examining how ethical principles, theories, and guidelines inform the design, implementation, and governance of AI systems. By examining the intersection of ethics and AI, we aim to understand how ethical frameworks can help address pressing ethical challenges and promote the responsible and ethical development of AI technologies. Through a comprehensive exploration of ethical considerations in AI, we can foster a deeper understanding of the ethical dimensions of AI research and practice and contribute to the development of AI systems that align with ethical principles, values, and goals.

Utilitarianism and AI Ethics

Utilitarianism is a consequentialist ethical theory that evaluates the morality of actions based on their outcomes or consequences, with the goal of maximizing overall happiness or utility and minimizing suffering or harm. In the context of Artificial Intelligence (AI) ethics, utilitarianism provides a framework for assessing the ethical implications of AI systems and guiding decisions to promote the greatest good for the greatest number of individuals. This chapter explores the principles of utilitarianism and its application to AI ethics, examining how utilitarian considerations can inform the development, deployment, and governance of AI technologies.

Principles of Utilitarianism:

Utilitarianism traces its roots back to philosophers such as Jeremy Bentham and John Stuart Mill, who argued that the morality of actions should be judged by their consequences in terms of pleasure or happiness and pain or suffering. The central tenet of utilitarianism is the principle of utility, which holds that actions are morally right if they produce the greatest amount of happiness or pleasure and minimize the greatest amount of pain or suffering for the greatest number of individuals.

Application of Utilitarianism to AI Ethics:

In the context of AI ethics, utilitarianism provides a framework for evaluating the ethical implications of AI systems based on their impact on human welfare and well-being. Utilitarian considerations can inform decisions about the design, deployment, and use of AI technologies to maximize overall social welfare and minimize negative consequences for individuals and communities. Some key areas where utilitarianism can be applied to AI ethics include:

1. **AI for Social Good:**

Utilitarianism encourages the development and deployment of AI technologies that have positive social impacts and promote the common good. AI applications in areas such as healthcare, education, environmental protection, and disaster response can be evaluated based on their ability to improve human welfare, enhance quality of life, and address pressing societal challenges. Utilitarian considerations may involve prioritizing AI projects that have the potential to save lives, reduce suffering, or improve access to essential services for marginalized communities.

2. Ethical AI Design:

Utilitarianism emphasizes the importance of designing AI systems that maximize benefits and minimize harms for all stakeholders involved. In the design phase, utilitarian considerations may involve identifying potential risks, biases, and unintended consequences of AI technologies and implementing safeguards to mitigate these risks. For example, AI algorithms used in decision-making processes should be evaluated for fairness, transparency, and accountability to ensure that they do not discriminate against certain individuals or perpetuate social inequalities.

3. AI Policy and Regulation:

Utilitarianism can inform AI policy and regulation by guiding decisions that maximize overall social welfare and minimize negative impacts on individuals and society. Utilitarian considerations may involve balancing competing interests, values, and priorities to develop policies that promote innovation, competition, and economic growth while protecting public safety, privacy, and human rights. Policymakers may use utilitarian principles to assess the risks and benefits of AI technologies and implement regulatory frameworks that encourage responsible AI development and deployment.

4. Ethical Decision Making in AI Systems:

Utilitarianism provides a framework for making ethical decisions within AI systems, such as autonomous vehicles, predictive analytics, and recommendation systems. AI algorithms can be programmed to prioritize actions that maximize overall utility, taking into account factors such as safety, efficiency, and fairness. For example, autonomous vehicles may be programmed to minimize the number of accidents and casualties on the road, while predictive analytics systems may prioritize interventions that improve public health outcomes or reduce crime rates.

Challenges and Limitations:

While utilitarianism offers valuable insights into AI ethics, it also poses certain challenges and limitations that must be addressed. One challenge is the difficulty of accurately predicting the long-term consequences of AI technologies and assessing their impact on diverse stakeholders. Utilitarian calculations may also be influenced by biases, uncertainties, and subjective judgments, leading to disagreements about the appropriate course of action. Additionally, utilitarianism may prioritize aggregate welfare over individual rights and liberties, raising concerns about the potential for harm to minority groups or vulnerable populations.

Utilitarianism provides a valuable framework for addressing ethical considerations in AI ethics and guiding decisions to promote the greatest good for the greatest number of individuals. By applying utilitarian principles to the development, deployment, and governance of AI technologies, we can maximize the social benefits of AI while minimizing negative consequences for individuals and society. However, utilitarianism must be applied judiciously, taking into account the complexities and nuances of AI ethics and ensuring that ethical decisions are grounded in fairness, transparency, and respect for human rights and dignity. Through thoughtful ethical deliberation and responsible decision making, we can harness the transformative potential of AI to create a more just, equitable, and humane world.

Deontological Ethics and AI Decision Making

Deontological ethics, often associated with the moral philosophy of Immanuel Kant, emphasizes the importance of moral duties, principles, and rules in guiding ethical behavior. In the context of

Artificial Intelligence (AI) decision making, deontological ethics provides a framework for assessing the ethical implications of AI systems based on principles of duty, rights, and respect for persons. This chapter explores the principles of deontological ethics and its application to AI decision making, examining how deontological considerations can inform the development, deployment, and governance of AI technologies.

Principles of Deontological Ethics:

Deontological ethics posits that certain actions are inherently right or wrong, regardless of their consequences, based on principles of duty, rights, and respect for persons. The central tenet of deontological ethics is the concept of the categorical imperative, which emphasizes the importance of acting in accordance with universalizable rules or principles that respect the inherent dignity and autonomy of individuals. According to Kant, moral duties are derived from rational principles that apply universally to all rational beings, irrespective of their desires or interests.

Application of Deontological Ethics to AI Decision Making:

In the context of AI decision making, deontological ethics provides a framework for evaluating the ethical implications of AI systems based on principles of autonomy, dignity, and respect for human rights. Deontological considerations can inform decisions about the design, deployment, and use of AI technologies to ensure that they uphold fundamental moral principles and protect the rights and interests of individuals. Some key areas where deontological ethics can be applied to AI decision making include:

1. **Respect for Autonomy:**

Deontological ethics emphasizes the importance of respecting individual autonomy and agency in decision making. In the design and deployment of AI systems, deontological considerations may involve ensuring that users have the freedom to make informed choices and control over how their data is collected, processed, and used. AI systems should respect principles of informed consent, transparency, and user empowerment, allowing individuals to exercise their autonomy and make decisions that align with their values and preferences.

2. Duty to Protect Privacy and Confidentiality:

Deontological ethics emphasizes the duty to respect and protect the privacy and confidentiality of individuals' personal information. In the context of AI, this duty requires ensuring that AI systems adhere to ethical principles of data privacy, security, and confidentiality. AI algorithms should be designed and implemented in a way that minimizes the risk of unauthorized access, misuse, or disclosure of sensitive information and respects individuals' rights to privacy and data protection.

3. Principle of Nonmaleficence:

Deontological ethics includes the principle of nonmaleficence, which prohibits actions that cause harm or violate the rights of others. In the development and deployment of AI systems, this principle requires ensuring that AI technologies do not cause harm, discriminate against certain individuals or groups, or infringe on their rights and liberties. AI algorithms should be evaluated for fairness, accuracy, and bias to minimize the risk of harm and ensure that they treat all individuals with dignity and respect.

4. Principle of Justice and Fairness:

Deontological ethics emphasizes the principle of justice, which requires treating individuals with equal respect and dignity and ensuring fairness in decision making. In the context of AI, this principle requires addressing issues of bias, discrimination, and inequality in AI algorithms and decision-making processes. AI systems should be designed and implemented in a way that promotes fairness, equity, and inclusivity, and mitigates the risk of perpetuating or exacerbating social inequalities and injustices.

Challenges and Limitations:

While deontological ethics offers valuable insights into AI decision making, it also poses certain challenges and limitations that must be addressed. One challenge is the potential conflict between deontological principles and consequentialist considerations, such as the trade-off between individual rights and the overall welfare of society. Deontological ethics may also face challenges in reconciling conflicting duties or principles in complex ethical dilemmas, such as the tension between privacy and security in AI systems.

Deontological ethics provides a valuable framework for addressing ethical considerations in AI decision making and guiding decisions that respect individual autonomy, dignity, and rights. By applying deontological principles to the development, deployment, and governance of AI technologies, we can ensure that AI systems uphold fundamental moral principles and protect the rights and interests of individuals. However, deontological ethics must be applied judiciously, taking into account the complexities and nuances of AI decision making and ensuring that ethical decisions are grounded in principles of fairness, transparency, and respect for human dignity. Through thoughtful ethical deliberation and responsible decision making, we can harness the transformative potential of AI to create a more just, equitable, and humane world.

Virtue Ethics in AI Design and Implementation

Virtue ethics is a moral theory that emphasizes the importance of character, virtues, and moral excellence in guiding ethical behavior. In the context of Artificial Intelligence (AI) design and implementation, virtue ethics provides a framework for evaluating the ethical implications of AI systems based on the character and intentions of the individuals involved in their development, deployment, and use. This chapter explores the principles of virtue ethics and its application to AI design and implementation, examining how virtue ethical considerations can promote the development of AI systems that embody ethical values and contribute to the flourishing of individuals and society.

Principles of Virtue Ethics:

Virtue ethics traces its roots back to ancient Greek philosophers such as Aristotle, who argued that ethical behavior arises from the cultivation of virtuous character traits such as courage, honesty, compassion, and wisdom. According to virtue ethics, moral virtues are intrinsic goods that contribute to human flourishing and the good life, and individuals should strive to develop and embody these virtues in their actions and relationships. Virtue ethical theories focus on the moral agent rather than the actions themselves, emphasizing the importance of moral education, self-reflection, and the cultivation of virtuous habits.

Application of Virtue Ethics to AI Design and Implementation:

In the context of AI design and implementation, virtue ethics provides a framework for evaluating the ethical implications of AI systems based on the character and intentions of the individuals involved. Virtue ethical considerations can inform decisions about the design, deployment, and governance of AI technologies to ensure that they promote human flourishing, foster ethical behavior, and contribute to the common good. Some key areas where virtue ethics can be applied to AI design and implementation include:

1. Ethical Leadership and Responsibility:

Virtue ethics emphasizes the importance of ethical leadership and responsibility in guiding the development and deployment of AI technologies. Virtue ethical considerations may involve ensuring that AI researchers, engineers, and policymakers possess and cultivate virtuous character traits such as honesty, integrity, empathy, and accountability. Ethical leaders in the field of AI should demonstrate virtues such as wisdom, courage, and humility, and prioritize ethical considerations in decision making and practice.

2. Human-Centered Design and Values:

Virtue ethics promotes human-centered design and values in the development of AI systems, prioritizing the well-being, autonomy, and dignity of individuals. Virtue ethical considerations may involve incorporating ethical values such as fairness, transparency, and inclusivity into the design and implementation of AI technologies. AI systems should be designed to empower users, enhance human capabilities, and promote meaningful human-machine interaction, while respecting individual rights and preferences.

3. Ethical Use of AI:

Virtue ethics encourages the ethical use of AI technologies to promote human flourishing and the common good. Virtue ethical considerations may involve ensuring that AI systems are used responsibly and ethically in various domains, such as healthcare, education, finance, and criminal justice. AI applications should be evaluated for their potential impact on individuals and society, and decisions about their deployment and use should be guided by ethical principles such as beneficence, nonmaleficence, and justice.

4. Accountability and Transparency:

Virtue ethics emphasizes the importance of accountability and transparency in the design and implementation of AI systems. Virtue ethical considerations may involve ensuring that AI developers and organizations are transparent about their intentions, practices, and decision-making processes. AI systems should be accountable for their actions and outcomes, and mechanisms should be in place to address ethical concerns, respond to feedback, and mitigate risks associated with their use.

Challenges and Limitations:

While virtue ethics offers valuable insights into AI design and implementation, it also poses certain challenges and limitations that must be addressed. One challenge is the subjective nature of virtue ethical judgments, which may vary depending on cultural, social, and individual differences in values and beliefs. Virtue ethics may also face challenges in operationalizing and measuring virtuous character traits in AI systems, such as trustworthiness, empathy, and integrity.

Virtue ethics provides a valuable framework for addressing ethical considerations in AI design and implementation and promoting the development of AI systems that embody ethical values and contribute to human flourishing. By incorporating virtue ethical principles into the design, deployment, and governance of AI technologies, we can ensure that AI systems promote ethical behavior, empower individuals, and enhance the well-being of society. However, virtue ethics must be applied judiciously, taking into account the complexities and nuances of AI design and implementation, and ensuring that ethical decisions are grounded in principles of virtue, wisdom, and compassion. Through thoughtful ethical deliberation and responsible decision making, we can harness the transformative potential of AI to create a more just, equitable, and humane world.

Chapter 5
Bias and Fairness in Algorithmic Decision Making

In the age of Artificial Intelligence (AI), algorithms play an increasingly prominent role in decision making across various domains, from finance and healthcare to criminal justice and hiring. However, as AI systems become more pervasive, concerns about bias and fairness in algorithmic decision making have come to the forefront. Bias in AI algorithms can lead to discriminatory outcomes, perpetuate social inequalities, and undermine trust in automated systems. In this chapter, we delve into the complex issues surrounding bias and fairness in algorithmic decision making.

As AI technologies become increasingly integrated into our daily lives, the need to address bias and promote fairness in algorithmic decision making has become paramount. Algorithmic bias refers to systematic errors or unfairness in AI systems that result in discriminatory outcomes against certain individuals or groups. These biases can arise from various sources, including biased training data, algorithmic design choices, and socio-cultural factors. In this chapter, we will explore the different forms of bias in AI algorithms, the impact of biased decision making on individuals and society, and strategies for mitigating bias and promoting fairness in algorithmic systems. By understanding the complexities of bias and fairness in algorithmic decision making, we can work towards creating more equitable and just AI systems that serve the needs of all members of society.

Understanding Bias in AI Systems

In the realm of Artificial Intelligence (AI), the concept of bias has garnered significant attention due to its potential to perpetuate inequalities and discriminate against certain individuals or groups. Bias in AI systems refers to the systematic errors or prejudices that lead to unfair or discriminatory outcomes in decision making. As AI technologies become increasingly integrated into various aspects of society, understanding and addressing bias in AI systems has become paramount. This chapter aims to provide a comprehensive overview of bias in AI systems, exploring its sources, manifestations, impacts, and strategies for mitigation.

1. **Sources of Bias in AI Systems:**

Bias in AI systems can stem from various sources, including:

   a) **Biased Training Data:** One of the primary sources of bias in AI systems is biased training data. If the training data used to develop AI algorithms is not representative or contains inherent biases, the resulting algorithms may learn and perpetuate these biases in their decision-making processes.

   b) **Algorithmic Design Choices:** Bias can also be introduced through the design choices made during the development of AI algorithms. For example, if certain features or variables are given more weight or importance than others, it can lead to biased outcomes.

   c) **Socio-cultural Factors:** Bias in AI systems can reflect broader socio-cultural biases and prejudices prevalent in society. These biases may be embedded in the data used to train AI algorithms or the assumptions underlying the algorithmic models.

2. **Manifestations of Bias in AI Systems:**

Bias in AI systems can manifest in various ways, including:

a) **Discriminatory Outcomes:** Bias in AI algorithms can result in discriminatory outcomes, where certain individuals or groups are unfairly disadvantaged or marginalized based on their race, gender, age, or other protected characteristics.

b) **Disparate Impact:** AI systems may exhibit disparate impact, where certain groups are disproportionately affected by algorithmic decisions. For example, a facial recognition system may be less accurate in identifying individuals from minority racial groups compared to white individuals.

c) **Amplification of Existing Inequalities:** Bias in AI systems has the potential to amplify existing inequalities and disparities in society. For example, biased algorithms used in hiring or lending decisions may perpetuate historical patterns of discrimination and exclusion.

3. Impacts of Bias in AI Systems:

The impacts of bias in AI systems can be far-reaching and profound, affecting individuals, communities, and society as a whole. Some of the key impacts include:

a) **Inequitable Treatment:** Bias in AI systems can result in individuals being treated unfairly or discriminatorily, leading to negative consequences such as denial of opportunities, services, or resources.

b) **Erosion of Trust:** When AI systems produce biased or unfair outcomes, it can erode trust in these systems and undermine their credibility and legitimacy. This lack of trust can hinder the adoption and acceptance of AI technologies in various domains.

c) **Reinforcement of Stereotypes:** Biased AI algorithms have the potential to reinforce and perpetuate stereotypes and prejudices, further entrenching social inequalities and discrimination.

4. **Strategies for Mitigating Bias in AI Systems:**

Addressing bias in AI systems requires a multi-faceted approach that involves:

a) **Diverse and Representative Data:** Ensuring that AI algorithms are trained on diverse and representative data sets can help mitigate bias by reducing the likelihood of learning from biased or unrepresentative samples.

b) **Algorithmic Fairness Measures:** Incorporating fairness measures into the design and evaluation of AI algorithms can help identify and mitigate bias. These measures may include fairness constraints, bias detection algorithms, and fairness-aware training techniques.

c) **Transparency and Accountability:** Promoting transparency and accountability in the development and deployment of AI systems can help mitigate bias by enabling stakeholders to understand how algorithms make decisions and hold developers accountable for biased outcomes.

d) **Ethical Oversight and Regulation:** Implementing ethical oversight mechanisms and regulatory frameworks can help ensure that AI systems are developed and deployed in accordance with ethical principles and values, including fairness, equity, and non-discrimination.

e) **Continuous Monitoring and Evaluation:** Regularly monitoring and evaluating AI systems for bias and discriminatory outcomes is essential for identifying and addressing bias in real-time. This may involve ongoing testing, validation, and auditing of AI algorithms throughout their lifecycle.

Bias in AI systems is a complex and multifaceted issue that requires careful consideration and proactive measures to address. By understanding the sources, manifestations, and impacts of bias in AI systems, and implementing strategies for mitigation, we can work towards creating more equitable, inclusive, and just AI technologies that serve the needs of all members of society. As AI continues to play an increasingly prominent role in various domains, it is essential to prioritize fairness, transparency, and accountability in the development and deployment of AI systems to ensure that they uphold fundamental ethical principles and promote the well-being of individuals and communities.

Fairness Metrics and Evaluation Techniques in AI Systems

As Artificial Intelligence (AI) systems become more prevalent in decision-making processes across various domains, ensuring fairness and mitigating biases in these systems has become a crucial area of concern. Fairness metrics and evaluation techniques play a vital role in assessing the fairness of AI algorithms and models, identifying potential biases, and guiding efforts to mitigate them. This chapter aims to provide a comprehensive overview of fairness metrics and evaluation techniques in AI systems, exploring their principles, applications, and challenges.

1. Understanding Fairness in AI Systems:

Fairness in AI systems refers to the absence of bias or discrimination in algorithmic decision making, ensuring that individuals are treated equitably and impartially regardless of their characteristics or background. However, achieving fairness in AI systems is complex due to the myriad of factors that can introduce biases, including biased training data, algorithmic design choices, and socio-cultural influences. Fairness metrics and evaluation techniques are essential tools for assessing the fairness of AI systems and identifying areas for improvement.

2. Types of Fairness Metrics:

Fairness metrics are quantitative measures used to evaluate the fairness of AI algorithms and models across different demographic groups or protected characteristics. Several types of fairness metrics are commonly used in the evaluation of AI systems, including:

a) **Group Fairness Metrics:** Group fairness metrics assess the distribution of outcomes or predictions across different demographic groups, such as race, gender, or age. Common group fairness metrics include:

- **Statistical Parity:** Also known as demographic parity, statistical parity measures whether the outcomes of an algorithm are distributed equally across different groups. It compares the proportion of positive outcomes (e.g., loan approvals) for each group to ensure no group is systematically disadvantaged.

- **Equal Opportunity:** Equal opportunity measures whether the true positive rate (TPR) or recall is equal across different groups, ensuring that the algorithm does not disproportionately favor one group over another in terms of correctly identifying positive instances.

- **Equalized Odds:** Equalized odds measures whether both the true positive rate (TPR) and false positive rate (FPR) are equal across different groups, ensuring that the algorithm makes equally accurate predictions for all groups while avoiding disparate error rates.

b) **Individual Fairness Metrics:** Individual fairness metrics assess whether similar individuals receive similar outcomes or predictions from the algorithm, regardless of their characteristics. Common individual fairness metrics include:

- **Calibration:** Calibration measures the agreement between predicted probabilities and observed outcomes for individuals with similar predicted scores. It ensures that the probability estimates provided by the algorithm are well-calibrated and reliable across different groups.

- **Treatment Equality:** Treatment equality measures whether individuals who are similar in terms of their relevant features receive similar treatments or decisions from the algorithm, ensuring consistency and fairness in decision making.

3. Evaluation Techniques for Fairness:

In addition to fairness metrics, various evaluation techniques are used to assess the fairness of AI systems and identify biases. Some commonly used evaluation techniques include:

a) **Fairness Testing:** Fairness testing involves evaluating the performance of AI algorithms across different demographic groups or sensitive attributes to identify disparities or biases. It may involve testing the algorithm with synthetic data generated to represent different demographic groups or perturbing the input data to simulate variations in demographic characteristics.

b) **Counterfactual Explanations:** Counterfactual explanations involve generating alternative scenarios or outcomes to understand how changes in input features would affect the algorithm's predictions. By comparing the predicted outcomes with and without certain attributes or characteristics, counterfactual explanations can help identify biases and disparities in algorithmic decision making.

c) **Adversarial Testing:** Adversarial testing involves testing the resilience of AI algorithms to adversarial attacks or manipulations designed to exploit vulnerabilities and introduce biases. Adversarial testing can help uncover weaknesses in the algorithm's decision boundaries and identify potential sources of bias or discrimination.

4. **Challenges and Considerations:**

Despite the importance of fairness metrics and evaluation techniques, several challenges and considerations must be addressed:

a) **Contextual Sensitivity:** Fairness metrics and evaluation techniques must be sensitive to the context and domain-specific considerations of AI applications. What constitutes fairness may vary depending on the societal norms, legal requirements, and ethical principles governing a particular domain.

b) **Trade-offs and Conflicting Objectives:** Achieving fairness in AI systems may involve trade-offs with other objectives, such as accuracy, efficiency, and utility. Balancing competing objectives while ensuring fairness requires careful consideration and may involve making explicit trade-offs between different fairness criteria.

c) **Dynamic and Evolving Nature:** Fairness metrics and evaluation techniques must be adaptable to the dynamic and evolving nature of AI systems. As AI algorithms and models are continuously updated and refined, fairness assessments must be ongoing and iterative to capture changes in performance and address emerging biases.

d) **Interpretability and Explainability:** Fairness metrics and evaluation techniques should be interpretable and explainable to stakeholders, including developers, policymakers, and end-users. Transparent and understandable fairness assessments are essential for fostering trust, accountability, and transparency in AI systems.

Fairness metrics and evaluation techniques are indispensable tools for assessing the fairness of AI systems, identifying biases, and guiding efforts to mitigate them. By leveraging these metrics and techniques, stakeholders can ensure that AI algorithms and models are developed and deployed in a manner that upholds principles of fairness, equity, and justice. However, addressing bias and promoting fairness in AI systems requires ongoing research, collaboration, and commitment to ethical principles and values. Through concerted efforts and multidisciplinary approaches, we can strive towards creating AI systems that serve the needs of all individuals and promote societal well-being.

Addressing Bias and Promoting Fairness in AI Algorithms

In recent years, the rise of Artificial Intelligence (AI) has brought unprecedented advancements in various domains, from healthcare and finance to education and criminal justice. However, alongside these advancements, concerns about bias and fairness in AI algorithms have become increasingly prominent. Bias in AI algorithms can lead to discriminatory outcomes, perpetuate social inequalities, and undermine trust in automated decision-making systems. Addressing bias and promoting fairness in AI algorithms is essential to ensure equitable treatment and mitigate the potential harms associated with biased decision-making. This chapter provides a comprehensive overview of strategies for addressing bias and promoting fairness in AI algorithms, exploring both technical and non-technical approaches.

1. Understanding Bias in AI Algorithms:

Bias in AI algorithms refers to systematic errors or prejudices that result in unfair or discriminatory outcomes in decision-making processes. Bias can arise from various sources, including biased training data, algorithmic design choices, and socio-cultural factors. Common types of bias in AI algorithms include:

- **Sampling Bias:** Biased training data that does not accurately represent the diversity of the population can lead to sampling bias, where certain groups are overrepresented or underrepresented in the data.

- **Algorithmic Bias:** Biases can also be introduced through the design and implementation of AI algorithms, such as the choice of features or the optimization criteria used.

- **Socio-cultural Bias:** AI algorithms may reflect and perpetuate broader socio-cultural biases and prejudices prevalent in society, leading to discriminatory outcomes.

2. **Technical Approaches for Addressing Bias:**

    a) **Fair Representation Learning:** Fair representation learning techniques aim to learn representations of data that are invariant to sensitive attributes such as race or gender. By disentangling the sensitive attributes from other features, these techniques can help mitigate bias in AI algorithms.

    b) **Fair Classification:** Fair classification methods aim to ensure fairness in algorithmic decision-making by optimizing for fairness constraints or incorporating fairness-aware regularization techniques. These methods strive to achieve equitable outcomes across different demographic groups while maintaining predictive accuracy.

    c) **Bias Detection and Mitigation:** Bias detection techniques involve analyzing AI algorithms for signs of bias or disparate impact across different groups. Once bias is detected, mitigation techniques such as reweighing, re-sampling, or adjusting decision thresholds can be applied to mitigate bias and promote fairness.

3. **Non-technical Approaches for Promoting Fairness:**

    a) **Diverse and Inclusive Teams:** Building diverse and inclusive teams that represent a wide range of perspectives and backgrounds can help mitigate bias in AI algorithms. By bringing together individuals with diverse experiences and expertise, teams can identify and address biases that may be overlooked by homogeneous groups.

    b) **Ethical Guidelines and Best Practices:** Establishing ethical guidelines and best practices for the development and deployment of AI algorithms can help promote fairness and mitigate bias. These guidelines may include principles such as transparency, accountability, and fairness, guiding developers and practitioners in ethical decision-making.

    c) **Stakeholder Engagement and Transparency:** Engaging with stakeholders, including end-users, policymakers, and affected communities, can help promote transparency and accountability in AI algorithms. By involving stakeholders in the development and deployment process, developers can ensure that AI algorithms reflect the values and preferences of the people they are designed to serve.

4. **Evaluating Fairness in AI Algorithms:**

    a) **Fairness Metrics:** Fairness metrics are quantitative measures used to evaluate the fairness of AI algorithms across different demographic groups or protected characteristics. Common fairness metrics include statistical parity, equal opportunity, and equalized odds, which assess the distribution of outcomes or predictions across different groups.

b) **Fairness Testing:** Fairness testing involves evaluating the performance of AI algorithms across different demographic groups or sensitive attributes to identify disparities or biases. It may involve testing the algorithm with synthetic data generated to represent different demographic groups or perturbing the input data to simulate variations in demographic characteristics.

5. Challenges and Considerations:

Addressing bias and promoting fairness in AI algorithms is a complex and multifaceted endeavor that poses several challenges and considerations:

a) **Trade-offs Between Fairness and Performance:** Achieving fairness in AI algorithms may involve trade-offs with other objectives, such as accuracy, efficiency, and utility. Balancing competing objectives while ensuring fairness requires careful consideration and may involve making explicit trade-offs between different fairness criteria.

b) **Interpretable and Explainable AI:** Promoting transparency and interpretability in AI algorithms is essential for understanding how decisions are made and identifying potential sources of bias. Interpretability techniques such as model explanations and feature importance analysis can help stakeholders understand the factors contributing to algorithmic decisions.

c) **Dynamic and Evolving Nature of Bias:** Bias in AI algorithms is dynamic and evolving, requiring ongoing monitoring and evaluation to detect and mitigate emerging biases. As AI algorithms are continuously updated and refined, fairness assessments must be iterative and adaptive to capture changes in performance and address emerging biases.

Addressing bias and promoting fairness in AI algorithms is essential to ensure equitable treatment and mitigate the potential harms associated with biased decision-making. By leveraging technical and non-technical approaches, stakeholders can work together to identify, mitigate, and prevent bias in AI algorithms, promoting fairness and accountability in automated decision-making systems. However, addressing bias in AI algorithms requires ongoing research, collaboration, and commitment to ethical principles and values. Through concerted efforts and multidisciplinary approaches, we can strive towards creating AI algorithms that uphold principles of fairness, equity, and justice, serving the needs of all individuals and promoting societal well-being.

Chapter 6
Transparency and Accountability in AI Systems

Transparency and accountability are essential pillars in the development and deployment of Artificial Intelligence (AI) systems. As AI technologies increasingly influence various aspects of society, understanding how these systems make decisions and ensuring accountability for their actions are critical for fostering trust, mitigating risks, and promoting ethical use. In this chapter, we delve into the significance of transparency and accountability in AI systems, exploring their roles in ensuring fairness, preventing harm, and upholding ethical standards. By examining the principles, challenges, and strategies associated with transparency and accountability, we aim to provide insights into how stakeholders can promote responsible AI development and deployment while addressing concerns related to bias, discrimination, and opacity. Through transparency and accountability, we can enhance the reliability, trustworthiness, and societal acceptance of AI systems, ultimately fostering a more inclusive and equitable AI ecosystem.

Importance of Transparency in AI Decision Making

Transparency in AI decision making is crucial for fostering trust, accountability, and ethical use of Artificial Intelligence (AI) systems. Transparency refers to the degree to which the inner workings, processes, and outcomes of AI algorithms are accessible, understandable, and explainable to stakeholders, including developers, users, and affected individuals or communities

1. **Fostering Trust and Confidence**

Transparency in AI decision making fosters trust and confidence among stakeholders by providing insights into how AI algorithms make decisions and the factors influencing their outcomes. When users understand how AI systems work and the rationale behind their decisions, they are more likely to trust the technology and feel confident in its reliability and fairness.

2. **Ensuring Accountability and Responsibility:**

Transparency in AI decision making is essential for ensuring accountability and responsibility among developers, organizations, and other stakeholders involved in the development and deployment of AI systems. By making the decision-making processes and criteria transparent, stakeholders can be held accountable for the outcomes of AI algorithms, whether they be positive or negative.

3. **Promoting Fairness and Equity:**

Transparency in AI decision making is critical for promoting fairness and equity in algorithmic outcomes. When the decision-making processes of AI systems are transparent, it becomes easier to identify and mitigate biases, discrimination, and other unfair practices that may lead to disparate outcomes for certain individuals or groups.

4. **Preventing Harm and Discrimination:**

Transparency in AI decision making helps prevent harm and discrimination by enabling stakeholders to identify and address potential risks and biases in algorithmic systems. When the inner workings of AI algorithms are opaque, it becomes challenging to detect and mitigate harmful behaviors or unintended consequences, leading to potential harm to individuals or communities.

5. **Enhancing User Understanding and Control:**

Transparency in AI decision making enhances user understanding and control by providing users with insights into how AI systems make decisions and the factors influencing their outcomes. When users have access to transparent explanations of algorithmic decisions, they can better understand and interpret the results, leading to more informed decision-making and greater user empowerment.

6. **Facilitating Compliance with Regulations and Standards:**

Transparency in AI decision making facilitates compliance with regulations, standards, and ethical guidelines governing the development and deployment of AI systems. Many regulatory frameworks and industry standards require transparency in algorithmic decision making to ensure accountability, fairness, and compliance with legal and ethical requirements.

7. **Building Public Acceptance and Legitimacy:**

Transparency in AI decision making is essential for building public acceptance and legitimacy of AI technologies. When the decision-making processes of AI systems are transparent and understandable, stakeholders are more likely to accept and trust the technology, leading to greater adoption and societal acceptance of AI systems.

8. **Encouraging Responsible Innovation and Governance:**

Transparency in AI decision making encourages responsible innovation and governance by promoting open dialogue, collaboration, and scrutiny among stakeholders. When the inner workings of AI algorithms are transparent, it becomes easier to identify potential risks, address ethical concerns, and develop appropriate safeguards to ensure responsible AI development and deployment.

Transparency in AI decision making is essential for fostering trust, accountability, and ethical use of AI systems. By making the decision-making processes and outcomes of AI algorithms transparent, stakeholders can promote fairness, prevent harm, and uphold ethical standards in AI development and deployment. Transparency not only enhances user understanding and control but also facilitates compliance with regulations and standards, builds public acceptance and legitimacy, and encourages responsible innovation and governance. As AI technologies continue to evolve and influence various aspects of society, ensuring transparency in AI decision making will remain a critical priority for promoting trust, fairness, and accountability in the AI ecosystem.

Accountability Mechanisms in AI Systems

As Artificial Intelligence (AI) becomes increasingly integrated into various aspects of society, ensuring accountability for AI systems has become a critical concern. Accountability mechanisms in AI systems are essential for holding developers, organizations, and other stakeholders responsible for the design, deployment, and outcomes of AI algorithms. In this chapter, we explore the importance of accountability in AI systems, examining the role of accountability mechanisms in promoting transparency, fairness, and ethical use of AI technologies.

1. Importance of Accountability in AI Systems:

Accountability in AI systems is essential for several reasons:

a) **Ensuring Responsible Use:** Accountability mechanisms hold developers and organizations responsible for the ethical use of AI technologies, ensuring that AI systems are deployed in a manner that upholds societal values and respects individual rights.

b) **Building Trust and Confidence:** Accountability promotes trust and confidence in AI systems by demonstrating a commitment to transparency, fairness, and ethical standards. When stakeholders are held accountable for the outcomes of AI algorithms, users are more likely to trust the technology and feel confident in its reliability and fairness.

c) **Preventing Harm and Discrimination:** Accountability mechanisms help prevent harm and discrimination by holding stakeholders accountable for the potential risks and biases associated with AI systems. By fostering accountability, stakeholders are incentivized to mitigate risks, address biases, and prevent unintended consequences that may harm individuals or communities.

d) **Promoting Transparency and Explainability:** Accountability mechanisms encourage transparency and explainability in AI systems by requiring developers to provide clear and understandable explanations of algorithmic decisions. When stakeholders are held accountable for the outcomes of AI algorithms, they are more likely to invest in transparency measures and ensure that decision-making processes are transparent and understandable to users.

2. **Types of Accountability Mechanisms:**

Several types of accountability mechanisms can be implemented to promote accountability in AI systems:

a) **Legal and Regulatory Frameworks:** Legal and regulatory frameworks establish clear guidelines and standards for the responsible development and deployment of AI technologies. These frameworks may include laws, regulations, and guidelines governing data privacy, discrimination, transparency, and accountability in AI systems.

b) **Ethical Guidelines and Best Practices:** Ethical guidelines and best practices provide voluntary standards and principles for developers and organizations to follow in the development and deployment of AI technologies. These guidelines may be developed by industry associations, professional organizations, or academic institutions and serve as a framework for ethical decision-making and responsible use of AI systems.

c) **Auditing and Certification Processes:** Auditing and certification processes involve third-party evaluation and assessment of AI systems to ensure compliance with legal, ethical, and technical standards. Independent auditors or certification bodies evaluate AI systems against predetermined criteria and issue certifications or reports documenting their findings.

d) **Transparency and Accountability Reports:** Transparency and accountability reports provide stakeholders with insights into the inner workings, processes, and outcomes of AI algorithms. These reports may include information on data collection and usage, algorithmic design choices, decision-making processes, and potential biases or risks associated with AI systems.

e) **Oversight and Governance Structures:** Oversight and governance structures establish mechanisms for monitoring, oversight, and governance of AI technologies. These structures may include government agencies, industry consortia, or independent bodies responsible for regulating and overseeing the development and deployment of AI systems.

3. **Challenges and Considerations:**

Implementing accountability mechanisms in AI systems poses several challenges and considerations:

   a) **Complexity and Opacity of AI Algorithms:** AI algorithms are often complex and opaque, making it challenging to understand how decisions are made and who is responsible for their outcomes. Ensuring accountability for AI systems requires transparency and explainability measures to make decision-making processes more accessible and understandable to stakeholders.

   b) **Bias and Discrimination:** Addressing bias and discrimination in AI algorithms is essential for ensuring fairness and accountability. However, identifying and mitigating biases in AI systems requires robust accountability mechanisms, including auditing, transparency, and oversight, to hold stakeholders accountable for biased outcomes.

   c) **Cross-border and Interdisciplinary Collaboration:** AI technologies are developed and deployed across borders and disciplines, making it challenging to establish consistent accountability mechanisms globally. Promoting accountability in AI systems requires cross-border and interdisciplinary collaboration among stakeholders, including governments, industry, academia, and civil society.

   d) **Balancing Innovation and Regulation:** Balancing innovation and regulation is essential for promoting responsible AI development and deployment. Accountability mechanisms should support innovation and technological advancement while ensuring compliance with legal, ethical, and societal norms.

Accountability mechanisms play a crucial role in promoting transparency, fairness, and ethical use of AI technologies. By holding developers, organizations, and other stakeholders accountable for the design, deployment, and outcomes of AI algorithms, accountability mechanisms foster trust, prevent harm, and promote responsible innovation. However, implementing effective accountability mechanisms in AI systems requires addressing challenges related to complexity, bias, cross-border collaboration, and balancing innovation with regulation. Through collaborative efforts and multidisciplinary approaches, stakeholders can work together to promote accountability in AI systems and ensure that AI technologies serve the needs of society while upholding ethical standards and values.

Challenges and Solutions in Ensuring Transparency and Accountability in AI Systems

As Artificial Intelligence (AI) technologies continue to advance and become more pervasive in various domains, ensuring transparency and accountability has emerged as a critical challenge. Transparency and accountability are essential for fostering trust, mitigating risks, and promoting ethical use of AI systems. However, achieving transparency and accountability in AI systems presents several challenges, ranging from technical complexities to ethical considerations. In this chapter, we explore the key challenges and propose solutions to ensure transparency and accountability in AI systems.

1. Technical Complexity and Opacity:

One of the primary challenges in ensuring transparency and accountability in AI systems is the technical complexity and opacity of AI algorithms. Many AI models, such as deep neural networks, are highly complex and opaque, making it challenging to understand how decisions are made and why certain outcomes are produced.

Solution: Develop Explainable AI (XAI) Techniques

Explainable AI (XAI) techniques aim to increase the transparency and interpretability of AI algorithms by providing human-understandable explanations of their decisions. These techniques include model-agnostic methods such as feature importance analysis, local explanations, and post-hoc explanations, which help users understand the factors influencing algorithmic decisions.

2. Bias and Discrimination:

Bias and discrimination in AI algorithms pose significant challenges to transparency and accountability. Biased training data, algorithmic design choices, and socio-cultural factors can all contribute to biased outcomes, leading to unfair treatment and discrimination against certain individuals or groups.

Solution: Implement Bias Detection and Mitigation Techniques

To address bias and discrimination in AI systems, it is essential to implement bias detection and mitigation techniques. These techniques involve analyzing AI algorithms for signs of bias and unfairness and taking corrective actions to mitigate bias and promote fairness. Techniques such as bias-aware training, fairness constraints, and fairness-aware regularization can help identify and mitigate biases in AI algorithms.

3. Lack of Standardized Metrics and Evaluation Techniques:

Another challenge in ensuring transparency and accountability in AI systems is the lack of standardized metrics and evaluation techniques for assessing algorithmic transparency, fairness, and accountability. Without clear metrics and evaluation methods, it becomes difficult to measure and compare the transparency and accountability of different AI systems.

Solution: Develop Standardized Transparency and Accountability Metrics

To address this challenge, stakeholders must work together to develop standardized transparency and accountability metrics and evaluation techniques for AI systems. These metrics should cover various aspects of algorithmic transparency, fairness, and accountability, such as explainability, bias detection, and impact assessment. By establishing clear standards and guidelines, stakeholders can ensure consistency and comparability in assessing the transparency and accountability of AI systems.

4. Cross-Border and Interdisciplinary Collaboration:

Ensuring transparency and accountability in AI systems requires cross-border and interdisciplinary collaboration among stakeholders from different countries, industries, and academic disciplines. However, coordinating collaboration and harmonizing practices across borders and disciplines can be challenging due to differences in legal frameworks, cultural norms, and technical standards.

Solution: Foster Collaborative Networks and Partnerships

To overcome this challenge, stakeholders should foster collaborative networks and partnerships to facilitate cross-border and interdisciplinary collaboration on transparency and accountability in AI systems. Collaborative initiatives such as international research consortia, industry alliances, and academic partnerships can promote knowledge sharing, best practices exchange, and capacity building across borders and disciplines.

5. Ethical Considerations and Societal Impacts:

Ensuring transparency and accountability in AI systems raises ethical considerations and societal impacts, such as privacy violations, autonomy infringements, and exacerbation of social inequalities. Addressing these concerns requires careful consideration of ethical principles, human rights, and societal values in the design, deployment, and governance of AI technologies.

Solution: Incorporate Ethical Frameworks and Impact Assessments

To address ethical considerations and societal impacts, stakeholders should incorporate ethical frameworks and impact assessments into the development and deployment of AI systems. Ethical frameworks provide guiding principles and values for ethical decision-making, while impact assessments help identify and mitigate potential risks and harms associated with AI technologies. By integrating ethical considerations and impact assessments into AI governance frameworks, stakeholders can promote responsible and ethical use of AI systems.

Ensuring transparency and accountability in AI systems is essential for fostering trust, promoting fairness, and mitigating risks associated with AI technologies. However, achieving transparency and accountability poses several challenges, including technical complexity, bias and discrimination, lack of standardized metrics, cross-border collaboration, and ethical considerations. By implementing solutions such as explainable AI techniques, bias detection and mitigation, standardized metrics, collaborative networks, and ethical frameworks, stakeholders can address these challenges and ensure that AI systems are transparent, accountable, and aligned with societal values and ethical principles. Through collaborative efforts and multidisciplinary approaches, we can build a more transparent, accountable, and ethically responsible AI ecosystem that serves the needs of society while upholding fundamental rights and values.

Chapter 7
Privacy and Data Ethics in the Digital Age

In the digital age, where data has become a ubiquitous currency driving innovation and economic growth, the importance of privacy and data ethics has come to the forefront. This chapter delves into the intricate landscape of privacy and data ethics, exploring the complexities, challenges, and ethical considerations surrounding the collection, use, and protection of personal data in an increasingly connected world.

As technology continues to evolve, so do the ethical dilemmas surrounding privacy and data ethics. From concerns about data breaches and surveillance to questions about consent and algorithmic bias, navigating the ethical terrain of data-driven technologies requires careful examination of ethical principles, legal frameworks, and societal norms.

In this chapter, we explore the multifaceted nature of privacy and data ethics, examining the implications of data collection and analysis on individual rights, societal values, and democratic principles. We also delve into the ethical responsibilities of technology developers, policymakers, and users in safeguarding privacy, promoting data transparency, and upholding ethical standards in the digital ecosystem.

Through critical analysis and discussion, this chapter aims to shed light on the complex interplay between technology, ethics, and privacy, and to provide insights into the ethical considerations and challenges shaping the future of data-driven innovation.

Privacy Concerns in AI Applications

As Artificial Intelligence (AI) continues to advance and permeate various aspects of society, privacy concerns have emerged as a significant ethical and regulatory issue. AI applications often rely on vast amounts of data, including personal information, to train algorithms and make predictions. However, the collection, use, and storage of this data raise fundamental questions about privacy rights, consent, and the potential for misuse. In this chapter, we explore the privacy concerns associated with AI applications, examining the implications for individuals, organizations, and society as a whole.

1. Data Collection and Surveillance:

One of the primary privacy concerns in AI applications is the collection and surveillance of personal data. AI systems often rely on large datasets to train algorithms and improve performance, leading to concerns about the indiscriminate collection of personal information without individuals' consent or awareness. Moreover, AI-enabled surveillance technologies, such as facial recognition and predictive analytics, raise concerns about mass surveillance, privacy invasion, and the erosion of civil liberties.

2. Data Breaches and Security Risks:

AI applications introduce new security risks and vulnerabilities that can compromise individuals' privacy and data security. Data breaches, unauthorized access, and cyberattacks pose significant threats to the confidentiality and integrity of personal information stored and processed by AI systems. Moreover, AI algorithms may inadvertently reveal sensitive information or patterns that can be exploited by malicious actors, leading to identity theft, financial fraud, or other forms of harm.

3. Algorithmic Bias and Discrimination:

Algorithmic bias and discrimination are pervasive privacy concerns in AI applications, particularly in contexts such as hiring, lending, and criminal justice. Biased training data, flawed algorithms, and socio-cultural biases embedded in AI systems can lead to discriminatory outcomes and perpetuate existing inequalities. Moreover, the opacity of AI algorithms and decision-making processes exacerbates concerns about accountability, transparency, and the potential for algorithmic discrimination.

4. Lack of Transparency and Explainability:

The lack of transparency and explainability in AI algorithms poses significant challenges to privacy protection and accountability. Many AI systems operate as black boxes, making it difficult for individuals to understand how decisions are made or why certain recommendations are provided. This opacity undermines individuals' ability to control their personal information and exercise their privacy rights, raising concerns about algorithmic accountability and the potential for hidden biases or errors.

5. Consent and User Control:

Privacy concerns in AI applications also relate to issues of consent and user control over personal data. Individuals may not always be aware of how their data is being collected, used, or shared by AI systems, leading to concerns about informed consent and autonomy. Moreover, AI algorithms may make decisions or recommendations based on personal data without individuals' explicit consent or understanding, raising questions about the adequacy of existing privacy frameworks and regulatory protections.

6. Regulatory and Ethical Challenges:

Addressing privacy concerns in AI applications requires navigating complex regulatory and ethical landscapes. Existing privacy laws and regulations, such as the General Data Protection Regulation (GDPR) in Europe and the California Consumer Privacy Act (CCPA) in the United States, provide a framework for protecting individuals' privacy rights and regulating data processing activities. However, the rapid pace of technological innovation and the global nature of AI applications pose challenges for effective enforcement and compliance with existing regulations.

7. Solutions and Mitigation Strategies:

To address privacy concerns in AI applications, stakeholders must adopt a multi-faceted approach that combines technological, regulatory, and ethical solutions:

a) **Privacy by Design:** Incorporate privacy considerations into the design and development of AI systems from the outset, ensuring that data protection principles such as data minimization, purpose limitation, and user consent are integrated into the design process.

b) **Transparency and Explainability:** Enhance the transparency and explainability of AI algorithms and decision-making processes to empower individuals to understand how their data is being used and make informed decisions about privacy risks.

c) **Ethical Guidelines and Frameworks:** Develop and adhere to ethical guidelines and frameworks for the responsible use of AI technologies, emphasizing principles such as fairness, accountability, and respect for individuals' privacy rights.

d) **Data Protection Mechanisms:** Implement robust data protection mechanisms, such as encryption, anonymization, and access controls, to safeguard personal data against unauthorized access, disclosure, or misuse.

e) **Regulatory Compliance:** Ensure compliance with relevant privacy laws and regulations governing AI applications, including requirements for data protection, consent management, and transparency reporting.

f) **Algorithmic Audits and Impact Assessments:** Conduct regular audits and impact assessments of AI algorithms to identify and mitigate potential privacy risks, biases, and discriminatory outcomes.

Privacy concerns in AI applications pose significant challenges for individuals, organizations, and society as a whole. Addressing these concerns requires a concerted effort to balance technological innovation with privacy protection, transparency, and accountability. By adopting privacy-by-design principles, enhancing transparency and explainability, adhering to ethical guidelines, implementing robust data protection mechanisms, and ensuring regulatory compliance, stakeholders can mitigate privacy risks and promote responsible and ethical use of AI technologies. Through collaborative efforts and collective action, we can build a more privacy-respecting and trustworthy AI ecosystem that respects individuals' privacy rights and upholds ethical standards in the digital age.

Data Ethics and Responsible Data Use

In the digital age, data has become a valuable resource driving innovation, economic growth, and societal progress. However, the widespread collection, analysis, and use of data raise ethical considerations and challenges related to privacy, fairness, transparency, and accountability. Data ethics, also known as responsible data use, refers to the principles, guidelines, and practices that govern the ethical use of data in various contexts, including research, business, governance, and technology development. In this chapter, we explore the importance of data ethics and responsible data use, examining the ethical considerations, challenges, and solutions associated with the collection, processing, and dissemination of data.

1. **Ethical Considerations in Data Use:**

    a) **Privacy:** Respecting individuals' privacy rights and ensuring the confidentiality and security of personal data are fundamental ethical considerations in data use. It is essential to obtain informed consent, minimize data collection, and protect sensitive information from unauthorized access or disclosure.

    b) **Fairness:** Ensuring fairness and equity in data use involves avoiding bias, discrimination, and unfair treatment in data collection, analysis, and decision-making processes. It is essential to address biases in data sources, algorithms, and decision models to prevent unjust outcomes and promote equal opportunities for all individuals.

    c) **Transparency:** Promoting transparency in data use involves providing clear and understandable explanations of data collection practices, data processing methods, and decision-making criteria to stakeholders. Transparency enhances trust, accountability, and informed decision-making, empowering individuals to understand how their data is being used and make informed choices.

    d) **Accountability:** Holding individuals, organizations, and institutions accountable for their actions and decisions regarding data use is essential for ensuring ethical conduct and mitigating potential harms. Accountability mechanisms such as audits, impact assessments, and regulatory oversight help identify and address ethical violations, promote responsible behavior, and uphold ethical standards.

2. **Challenges in Responsible Data Use:**

   a) **Data Quality:** Ensuring the quality, accuracy, and reliability of data is a significant challenge in responsible data use. Poor data quality, including inaccuracies, incompleteness, and bias, can undermine the integrity and trustworthiness of data-driven insights and decisions, leading to erroneous conclusions and harmful outcomes.

   b) **Data Privacy:** Protecting individuals' privacy rights and preventing unauthorized access or misuse of personal data pose challenges in responsible data use. The proliferation of data breaches, cyberattacks, and data mining techniques raises concerns about data privacy violations and the erosion of individuals' privacy rights in the digital age.

   c) **Algorithmic Bias:** Addressing bias and discrimination in algorithmic decision-making processes is a critical challenge in responsible data use. Biased training data, flawed algorithms, and socio-cultural biases embedded in AI systems can lead to discriminatory outcomes and perpetuate existing inequalities, posing ethical and legal risks.

   d) **Data Governance:** Establishing robust data governance frameworks and practices to ensure ethical data use and compliance with regulatory requirements is a complex challenge. Data governance involves defining policies, procedures, and standards for data management, access control, data sharing, and data protection across organizations and jurisdictions.

3. **Solutions and Best Practices:**

a) **Ethical Guidelines and Frameworks:** Adhering to ethical guidelines and frameworks for responsible data use, such as the Fair Information Practice Principles (FIPPs) and the European Union's General Data Protection Regulation (GDPR), helps organizations and individuals navigate ethical considerations and ensure compliance with legal and ethical standards.

b) **Privacy-Enhancing Technologies:** Implementing privacy-enhancing technologies, such as encryption, anonymization, and differential privacy, helps protect individuals' privacy rights and mitigate the risks of unauthorized access or disclosure of personal data.

c) **Bias Detection and Mitigation:** Employing bias detection and mitigation techniques, such as algorithmic audits, fairness-aware algorithms, and diverse and representative training data, helps identify and address biases in data sources, algorithms, and decision models, promoting fairness and equity in data use.

d) **Transparency and Accountability Measures:** Enhancing transparency and accountability measures, such as data transparency reports, algorithmic impact assessments, and independent audits, helps foster trust, accountability, and responsible behavior in data use, empowering stakeholders to understand and evaluate the ethical implications of data-driven decisions.

4. Promoting a Culture of Ethical Data Use:

Promoting a culture of ethical data use involves fostering awareness, education, and collaboration among stakeholders to prioritize ethical considerations and values in data-related activities. Organizations and institutions can promote ethical data use by providing training, resources, and support for ethical decision-making, promoting open dialogue and collaboration on ethical issues, and integrating ethical considerations into organizational policies, practices, and decision-making processes.

Data ethics and responsible data use are essential principles for navigating the ethical complexities and challenges of the digital age. By prioritizing privacy, fairness, transparency, and accountability in data-related activities, organizations, institutions, and individuals can uphold ethical standards, mitigate risks, and promote trust, integrity, and social responsibility in the use of data. Through collaborative efforts and collective action, we can build a more ethical and sustainable data ecosystem that respects individuals' rights, values, and dignity while harnessing the power of data for positive societal impact.

Regulatory Frameworks for Protecting Privacy in AI

As Artificial Intelligence (AI) technologies continue to advance and become increasingly integrated into various sectors, the need for robust regulatory frameworks to protect privacy has become more urgent. AI applications often rely on vast amounts of data, including personal information, raising concerns about privacy infringement, data misuse, and unauthorized access. In this chapter, we explore the regulatory frameworks designed to safeguard privacy in the context of AI, examining their scope, principles, challenges, and effectiveness in addressing emerging privacy concerns.

1. General Data Protection Regulation (GDPR):

The General Data Protection Regulation (GDPR), implemented by the European Union (EU) in 2018, is one of the most comprehensive and stringent privacy regulations globally. The GDPR aims to protect individuals' fundamental rights and freedoms regarding the processing of their personal data and to harmonize data protection laws across EU member states. Key principles of the GDPR include:

- **Lawfulness, Fairness, and Transparency:** Data processing must be lawful, fair, and transparent, with clear and explicit consent obtained from individuals for data collection and processing activities.

- **Purpose Limitation:** Personal data must be collected for specified, explicit, and legitimate purposes and not further processed in a manner incompatible with those purposes.

- **Data Minimization:** Data controllers must collect and process only the minimum amount of personal data necessary for the intended purpose, ensuring data accuracy, relevance, and timeliness.

- **Data Integrity and Confidentiality:** Personal data must be processed securely, ensuring its confidentiality, integrity, and availability, and protected against unauthorized access, disclosure, or alteration.

- **Accountability and Responsibility:** Data controllers and processors are accountable for complying with GDPR requirements, including implementing appropriate technical and organizational measures to ensure and demonstrate compliance.

The GDPR imposes significant obligations and responsibilities on organizations that process personal data, including AI developers, data controllers, and data processors. Non-compliance with GDPR requirements can result in severe penalties, including fines of up to €20 million or 4% of the organization's global annual turnover, whichever is higher.

2. **California Consumer Privacy Act (CCPA):**

The California Consumer Privacy Act (CCPA), enacted by the state of California in 2018, is one of the most comprehensive privacy laws in the United States. The CCPA grants California residents certain rights and protections regarding the collection, use, and sale of their personal information by businesses operating in California. Key provisions of the CCPA include:

- **Right to Know:** Individuals have the right to know what personal information businesses collect about them, the purposes for which it is used, and whether it is sold or disclosed to third parties.

- **Right to Opt-Out:** Individuals have the right to opt-out of the sale of their personal information to third parties and to request that businesses stop selling their personal data.

- **Right to Access:** Individuals have the right to access their personal information held by businesses and to request copies of their data in a readily usable format.

- Right to Deletion: Individuals have the right to request that businesses delete their personal information, subject to certain exceptions.

- Right to Non-Discrimination: Businesses are prohibited from discriminating against individuals who exercise their privacy rights under the CCPA, including by denying goods or services, charging different prices, or providing a different level of service.

The CCPA applies to businesses that meet certain thresholds, including those with annual gross revenues exceeding $25 million, those that buy, sell, or share personal information of 50,000 or more consumers, households, or devices, and those that derive 50% or more of their annual revenues from selling consumers' personal information.

3. Challenges and Limitations:

While regulatory frameworks such as the GDPR and CCPA provide important protections for individuals' privacy rights, they also face several challenges and limitations in the context of AI:

- **Complexity and Interpretation:** The GDPR and CCPA are complex regulations with numerous provisions and requirements, making compliance challenging for organizations, particularly those operating across multiple jurisdictions. Interpretation and application of regulatory requirements in the context of AI technologies, such as automated decision-making and algorithmic processing, can be ambiguous and subject to debate.

- **Technological Advancement:** The rapid pace of technological advancement, particularly in AI, presents challenges for regulatory frameworks to keep pace with evolving privacy risks and concerns. New AI applications and data processing techniques may pose novel privacy challenges that existing regulations are not adequately equipped to address.

- **Global Scope:** The GDPR and CCPA primarily apply to organizations operating within the EU and California, respectively, raising questions about their applicability to global companies and cross-border data transfers. Achieving regulatory harmonization and interoperability across different jurisdictions remains a significant challenge in the context of global data flows and international data transfers.

- **Enforcement and Compliance:** Enforcement of privacy regulations, such as the GDPR and CCPA, relies on regulatory authorities' capacity to investigate complaints, impose sanctions, and ensure compliance. However, resource constraints, jurisdictional limitations, and procedural hurdles may hinder effective enforcement and deterrence of privacy violations, particularly by multinational corporations.

4. Future Directions and Emerging Trends:

In response to evolving privacy concerns and technological developments, regulatory frameworks for protecting privacy in AI are likely to evolve and adapt in several ways:

- **Enhanced Accountability and Transparency:** Regulatory authorities may emphasize the importance of accountability and transparency in AI systems' design, development, and deployment, requiring organizations to demonstrate compliance with privacy regulations through transparent data processing practices, auditability, and documentation.

- **Ethical AI Guidelines:** Regulatory frameworks may incorporate ethical AI principles and guidelines, such as fairness, accountability, transparency, and non-discrimination, to promote responsible and ethical use of AI technologies while protecting individuals' privacy rights.

- **Data Protection by Design and Default:** Regulatory authorities may encourage organizations to implement privacy-enhancing technologies and practices, such as data protection by design and default, encryption, anonymization, and differential privacy, to minimize privacy risks and protect personal data from unauthorized access or disclosure.

- **International Cooperation:** Regulatory frameworks for protecting privacy in AI may increasingly emphasize international cooperation and collaboration among regulatory authorities, industry stakeholders, and civil society organizations to address global privacy challenges, harmonize standards, and promote interoperability across jurisdictions.

Regulatory frameworks play a crucial role in protecting individuals' privacy rights and promoting responsible data use in the context of AI. Regulations such as the GDPR and CCPA provide important protections for personal data, including provisions related to consent, transparency, data access, and accountability. However, regulatory frameworks face challenges and limitations in addressing emerging privacy concerns associated with AI technologies, such as algorithmic bias, data minimization, and cross-border data transfers. To address these challenges, regulatory authorities may need to enhance accountability, transparency, and ethical standards in AI systems' design and deployment while fostering international cooperation and collaboration to ensure effective privacy protection in the digital age. Through ongoing dialogue, engagement, and adaptation, regulatory frameworks can evolve to address the evolving privacy landscape and safeguard individuals' privacy rights in an increasingly data-driven world.

Chapter 8
AI and the Future of Work: Implications for Ethics

The integration of Artificial Intelligence (AI) technologies into the workforce is reshaping the landscape of employment, productivity, and economic growth. As AI systems automate tasks, augment human capabilities, and transform industries, ethical considerations arise regarding the impact on individuals, organizations, and society. In this chapter, we explore the implications of AI for the future of work through an ethical lens, examining the challenges, opportunities, and ethical dilemmas inherent in AI-driven workplace transformations.

AI technologies promise to enhance efficiency, innovation, and competitiveness in the workplace, offering opportunities for job creation, skills development, and economic prosperity. However, AI-driven automation and augmentation also raise concerns about job displacement, skill mismatches, and socioeconomic inequalities. Ethical considerations such as fairness, accountability, transparency, and human dignity are central to navigating the ethical dimensions of AI in the workplace.

Through critical analysis and discussion, this chapter aims to shed light on the ethical implications of AI for the future of work, exploring strategies for ensuring ethical AI adoption, promoting human-centric AI design, and addressing societal concerns about job displacement, reskilling, and social inclusion. By integrating ethical principles into AI deployment strategies and workplace policies, stakeholders can harness the transformative potential of AI technologies while upholding ethical standards and values in the evolving future of work landscape.

Impact of AI on Employment and Labor Practices

Artificial Intelligence (AI) technologies are revolutionizing industries across the globe, leading to significant changes in employment patterns and labor practices. While AI offers opportunities for increased productivity, efficiency, and innovation, its widespread adoption also raises concerns about job displacement, skills obsolescence, and the future of work. In this chapter, we explore the multifaceted impact of AI on employment and labor practices, examining the opportunities, challenges, and ethical considerations inherent in the AI-driven transformation of the workforce.

1. Automation and Job Displacement:

One of the most significant impacts of AI on employment is automation, where AI systems replace or augment human labor in various tasks and occupations. While automation can lead to increased efficiency and cost savings for businesses, it also raises concerns about job displacement and unemployment. Routine, repetitive tasks are particularly susceptible to automation, affecting industries such as manufacturing, transportation, and customer service. However, the extent of job displacement varies across industries and occupations, with some jobs being eliminated entirely, while others are transformed or created as a result of AI adoption.

2. Skill Requirements and Reskilling:

AI adoption reshapes the skill requirements and demands of the workforce, leading to a shift towards higher-skilled roles that require cognitive, creative, and interpersonal skills. As AI automates routine tasks, there is an increased demand for skills such as data analysis, problem-solving, and digital literacy. However, this shift also highlights the importance of reskilling and upskilling initiatives to ensure that workers are equipped with the necessary skills to adapt to changing job requirements. Investing in lifelong learning, training programs, and education pathways is essential to mitigate the risk of skills obsolescence and support workforce transition in the AI era.

3. Gig Economy and Alternative Work Arrangements:

AI technologies facilitate the growth of the gig economy and alternative work arrangements, enabling flexible, on-demand employment opportunities through platforms and digital marketplaces. While the gig economy offers flexibility and autonomy for workers, it also raises concerns about job insecurity, lack of benefits, and precarious working conditions. Additionally, AI-driven platforms may exacerbate inequalities and exploitation by algorithmically determining wages, assignments, and performance evaluations. Regulating the gig economy to ensure fair labor practices, social protections, and worker rights remains a challenge in the face of AI-driven disruptions.

4. Augmentation and Human-AI Collaboration:

Rather than replacing human workers, AI technologies often augment human capabilities, leading to new forms of human-AI collaboration in the workplace. AI systems can assist workers in tasks such as decision-making, problem-solving, and customer service, enhancing productivity and efficiency. However, ensuring effective collaboration between humans and AI requires addressing challenges such as trust, transparency, and accountability. Ethical considerations, such as bias detection, algorithmic fairness, and human oversight, are essential to prevent unintended consequences and ensure that AI complements rather than substitutes human labor.

5. Ethical Considerations and Labor Rights:

The widespread adoption of AI in the workplace raises ethical considerations and labor rights concerns regarding fairness, accountability, transparency, and workers' rights. Algorithmic decision-making, bias in AI systems, and data privacy issues can lead to discrimination, inequality, and infringement of labor rights. Additionally, AI-driven surveillance technologies, such as employee monitoring and performance tracking, raise concerns about privacy, autonomy, and workplace dignity. Ensuring ethical AI adoption and upholding labor rights requires regulatory frameworks, ethical guidelines, and stakeholder collaboration to promote responsible AI use, protect workers' rights, and mitigate potential harms.

6. Policy Responses and Regulatory Frameworks:

Addressing the impact of AI on employment and labor practices requires proactive policy responses and regulatory frameworks to ensure fairness, equity, and social inclusion. Governments, employers, and civil society organizations play a crucial role in shaping policies and practices that promote responsible AI adoption, support workforce transition, and protect labor rights. Initiatives such as universal basic income, job guarantee programs, and worker retraining schemes can help mitigate the negative effects of job displacement and support workers' transition to new employment opportunities in the AI-driven economy.

The impact of AI on employment and labor practices is multifaceted, with opportunities for increased productivity, innovation, and flexibility, as well as challenges related to job displacement, skills obsolescence, and ethical concerns. Navigating the AI-driven transformation of the workforce requires a comprehensive approach that balances technological advancement with social responsibility, ensuring that the benefits of AI are equitably distributed and that workers' rights are protected. By addressing the opportunities and challenges of AI in employment through ethical AI adoption, reskilling initiatives, and regulatory frameworks that prioritize fairness and inclusion, stakeholders can harness the transformative potential of AI while safeguarding the well-being and dignity of workers in the digital age.

Ethical Considerations in AI-driven Workplace Automation

In the contemporary landscape of technology integration, Artificial Intelligence (AI) is playing an increasingly prominent role in reshaping workplace dynamics. While AI-driven workplace automation promises enhanced efficiency and productivity, it also raises significant ethical considerations. This chapter delves into the nuanced ethical dimensions surrounding AI-driven workplace automation, exploring the implications, challenges, and principles guiding responsible implementation.

1. Job Displacement and Employment Impact:

AI-driven automation has the potential to disrupt traditional job roles and labor practices. While automation can lead to increased efficiency and cost savings for organizations, it may also result in job displacement for certain roles. Ethical considerations arise concerning the social and economic impact of job displacement, including questions of retraining, reskilling, and job transition support for affected workers. Organizations must balance the pursuit of technological advancement with ethical responsibilities to minimize adverse effects on employment and ensure equitable opportunities for all individuals within the workforce.

2. Algorithmic Bias and Fairness:

Algorithmic bias poses a significant ethical challenge in AI-driven workplace automation. AI systems are trained on historical data that may reflect biases present in society, leading to discriminatory outcomes. For instance, biased algorithms in hiring processes can perpetuate inequalities based on race, gender, or socioeconomic status. Ensuring fairness and equity in AI systems requires proactive measures to detect and mitigate biases throughout the algorithm's development and deployment stages. Ethical frameworks emphasizing fairness, transparency, and accountability are essential for promoting equitable outcomes in AI-driven workplace environments.

3. Transparency and Explainability:

Transparency and explainability are essential ethical principles in AI-driven workplace automation. Employees have the right to understand how AI systems make decisions that impact their work and livelihoods. Transparent AI systems provide clear explanations of their decision-making processes, enabling employees to trust and interpret algorithmic decisions accurately. Organizations must prioritize transparency and explainability to foster trust among employees and mitigate concerns related to algorithmic opacity and lack of accountability.

4. Human-AI Collaboration and Augmentation:

AI-driven workplace automation often involves human-AI collaboration, where AI systems augment human capabilities to enhance productivity and decision-making. Ethical considerations arise concerning the appropriate balance between human autonomy and AI assistance. It is crucial to maintain human agency and control in AI-driven work environments to prevent deskilling and dependency on AI systems. Ethical guidelines emphasizing human dignity, empowerment, and accountability guide responsible collaboration between humans and AI technologies in the workplace.

5. Data Privacy and Security:

Data privacy and security are paramount ethical considerations in AI-driven workplace automation. AI systems rely on vast amounts of data, including personal information, to make decisions and recommendations. Protecting the confidentiality, integrity, and availability of data is essential to uphold individuals' privacy rights and prevent unauthorized access or misuse of sensitive information. Organizations must adopt privacy-enhancing technologies and practices to safeguard personal data and mitigate privacy risks associated with AI-driven automation.

6. Ethical Decision-Making and Governance:

Ethical decision-making and governance frameworks are critical for ensuring responsible AI adoption in the workplace. Organizations must establish ethical guidelines, policies, and procedures that prioritize ethical principles such as fairness, transparency, and accountability. Ethical review boards and oversight committees play a crucial role in identifying and addressing ethical risks and dilemmas associated with AI-driven workplace automation. Additionally, fostering a culture of ethical awareness and dialogue among employees and stakeholders is essential for promoting responsible AI use and mitigating potential ethical challenges.

Ethical considerations in AI-driven workplace automation are complex and multifaceted, requiring careful attention and consideration from organizations and policymakers. By prioritizing ethical principles such as fairness, transparency, accountability, and human dignity, organizations can navigate the ethical complexities of AI deployment in the workplace responsibly. Through collaborative efforts and adherence to ethical guidelines, stakeholders can ensure that AI technologies are implemented in a manner that enhances productivity, innovation, and well-being for workers and society as a whole, while mitigating potential ethical risks and upholding fundamental human rights in the digital age.

Strategies for Ethical AI Adoption in the Workforce

As organizations increasingly integrate Artificial Intelligence (AI) technologies into their operations, ensuring ethical AI adoption in the workforce becomes paramount. Ethical AI adoption involves incorporating principles such as fairness, transparency, accountability, and human dignity into the development, deployment, and management of AI systems. This chapter explores strategies for ethical AI adoption in the workforce, focusing on initiatives that promote responsible AI use, mitigate potential risks, and uphold ethical standards.

1. Ethical Guidelines and Frameworks:

Establishing ethical guidelines and frameworks is a fundamental step towards ensuring ethical AI adoption in the workforce. Organizations should develop clear and comprehensive guidelines that outline ethical principles, guidelines, and best practices for AI development and deployment. These guidelines should address key ethical considerations such as fairness, transparency, accountability, and human rights. Additionally, organizations can leverage existing ethical frameworks, such as the IEEE Ethically Aligned Design, to inform their AI adoption strategies and ensure alignment with industry standards and best practices.

2. Ethical AI Design Principles:

Embedding ethical AI design principles into the development process is essential for ensuring that AI systems align with ethical values and principles. Ethical AI design principles emphasize human-centered design, fairness, transparency, and accountability throughout the AI lifecycle. Organizations should prioritize designing AI systems that are interpretable, explainable, and accountable, enabling users to understand how AI systems make decisions and identify potential biases or errors. Additionally, incorporating principles such as privacy by design and security by design helps mitigate risks and vulnerabilities associated with AI systems.

3. Fairness and Bias Mitigation:

Addressing fairness and mitigating bias in AI systems is critical for ensuring equitable outcomes in the workforce. Organizations should implement measures to detect, assess, and mitigate biases throughout the AI lifecycle, from data collection and preprocessing to algorithm development and deployment. Techniques such as bias detection, algorithmic auditing, and fairness-aware AI algorithms help identify and mitigate biases in AI systems, ensuring fair treatment and equal opportunities for all individuals. Additionally, organizations should prioritize diversity and inclusivity in data collection and model development to minimize the risk of biased outcomes.

4. Transparency and Explainability:

Promoting transparency and explainability in AI systems enhances trust, accountability, and user acceptance in the workforce. Organizations should prioritize designing AI systems that provide clear explanations of their decision-making processes, enabling users to understand how AI systems reach their conclusions. Techniques such as model interpretability, explanation generation, and transparency reports help users interpret and validate AI-driven decisions, fostering trust and confidence in AI technologies. Additionally, organizations should establish mechanisms for users to seek explanations or recourse in cases of algorithmic errors or unintended consequences.

5. Human Oversight and Control:

Maintaining human oversight and control is essential for ensuring accountability and ethical use of AI in the workforce. Organizations should establish mechanisms for human oversight and intervention in AI-driven decision-making processes, particularly in high-stakes or sensitive domains. Human-in-the-loop systems, where humans are involved in the decision-making loop alongside AI systems, enable users to monitor, validate, and override AI-driven decisions when necessary. Additionally, organizations should empower employees with the knowledge, skills, and resources to critically evaluate and challenge AI-driven decisions, promoting a culture of ethical awareness and accountability in the workforce.

6. **Continuous Monitoring and Evaluation:**

Continuous monitoring and evaluation of AI systems are essential for identifying and addressing ethical risks and challenges in the workforce. Organizations should implement robust monitoring and evaluation mechanisms to assess the performance, fairness, and impact of AI systems over time. Regular audits, impact assessments, and feedback mechanisms enable organizations to identify biases, errors, and unintended consequences in AI systems and take corrective actions to mitigate risks and improve performance. Additionally, organizations should establish channels for stakeholders to report ethical concerns or violations related to AI use, ensuring transparency and accountability in the workforce.

7. **Ethical Training and Education:**

Providing ethical training and education to employees is crucial for promoting responsible AI use and ethical decision-making in the workforce. Organizations should offer training programs, workshops, and resources that raise awareness of ethical considerations, principles, and best practices in AI adoption. Training should cover topics such as bias mitigation, fairness assessment, transparency, and accountability in AI systems, empowering employees to recognize and address ethical challenges in their work. Additionally, organizations should foster a culture of open dialogue and collaboration on ethical issues, encouraging employees to raise concerns and seek guidance on ethical dilemmas related to AI use.

8. Stakeholder Engagement and Collaboration:

Engaging stakeholders and fostering collaboration is essential for ensuring ethical AI adoption in the workforce. Organizations should involve employees, customers, regulators, and other relevant stakeholders in the AI development and deployment process, soliciting feedback, and input on ethical considerations and concerns. Collaborative initiatives such as industry partnerships, multi-stakeholder forums, and advisory boards enable organizations to leverage diverse perspectives and expertise to address ethical challenges and promote responsible AI use in the workforce.

Ethical AI adoption in the workforce requires a holistic approach that integrates ethical principles, guidelines, and practices into the development, deployment, and management of AI systems. By prioritizing fairness, transparency, accountability, and human dignity, organizations can navigate the ethical complexities of AI adoption and ensure that AI technologies are used responsibly to enhance productivity, innovation, and well-being in the workforce. Through collaborative efforts, continuous monitoring, and ethical training, stakeholders can promote a culture of ethical awareness and accountability that upholds ethical standards and values in the evolving landscape of AI-driven work environments.

Chapter 9
Autonomous Systems and Moral Responsibility

The emergence of autonomous systems, powered by Artificial Intelligence (AI) and robotics, introduces profound questions about moral responsibility in technological contexts. As these systems become increasingly autonomous, capable of making decisions and taking actions without human intervention, ethical considerations surrounding their behavior and accountability come to the forefront. This chapter delves into the intricate relationship between autonomous systems and moral responsibility, exploring the challenges, implications, and ethical frameworks that govern their actions.

Autonomous systems encompass a wide range of technologies, including self-driving cars, autonomous drones, and intelligent robots, each presenting unique ethical dilemmas. As these systems operate in complex environments, interacting with humans and making decisions with real-world consequences, questions arise regarding their capacity for moral agency and the allocation of responsibility for their actions. Understanding the ethical implications of autonomous systems requires examining issues such as algorithmic decision-making, human oversight, and the potential impact on societal norms and values.

By grappling with the ethical complexities of autonomous systems and moral responsibility, we can navigate the ethical challenges posed by these technologies and develop frameworks for responsible development and deployment. This chapter aims to stimulate critical reflection and dialogue on the ethical dimensions of autonomous systems, fostering a deeper understanding of their implications for society and informing ethical decision-making in the design, regulation, and use of autonomous technologies.

Understanding Autonomous Systems and Their Decision Making

Autonomous systems, encompassing a diverse array of technologies such as self-driving cars, drones, and robotic assistants, are revolutionizing various industries and aspects of everyday life. These systems possess the capability to make decisions and take actions without direct human intervention, raising important questions about their decision-making processes and the ethical considerations surrounding their actions. In this chapter, we delve into the intricacies of autonomous systems' decision making, exploring the underlying mechanisms, challenges, and ethical implications.

1. Autonomous Systems: A Brief Overview

Autonomous systems are technological marvels designed to perform tasks or make decisions with varying degrees of autonomy. These systems rely on sensors, algorithms, and actuators to perceive their environment, process information, and execute actions. From self-driving cars navigating city streets to autonomous drones conducting surveillance missions, these systems operate in complex and dynamic environments, often interacting with humans and other entities.

2. Decision Making in Autonomous Systems

The decision-making process in autonomous systems involves several stages, each influenced by factors such as sensor data, algorithms, objectives, and constraints.

- **Perception:** Autonomous systems gather information about their environment through sensors such as cameras, lidar, and radar. This sensory data is processed to create a representation of the system's surroundings, including objects, obstacles, and relevant features.

- **Planning:** Based on the perceived environment and predefined objectives, autonomous systems formulate a plan or course of action to achieve their goals. This planning process involves generating sequences of actions or trajectories that optimize performance while considering constraints such as resource limitations and safety requirements.

- **Decision Making:** Autonomous systems make decisions by evaluating potential actions or trajectories and selecting the most appropriate course of action based on predefined criteria. Decision-making algorithms may incorporate machine learning techniques to adapt to changing conditions and improve performance over time.

- **Execution:** Once a decision is made, autonomous systems execute the selected action or trajectory using actuators such as motors, actuators, or manipulators. Execution may involve feedback mechanisms to monitor and adjust the system's behavior in response to unforeseen events or deviations from the planned trajectory.

3. Challenges in Autonomous Decision Making

Despite their technological sophistication, autonomous systems face several challenges in decision making:

- **Uncertainty:** Autonomous systems must operate in uncertain and unpredictable environments, where sensory data may be noisy or incomplete, and external factors may change rapidly. Dealing with uncertainty requires robust decision-making algorithms that can adapt to unexpected circumstances and make informed decisions under uncertainty.

- **Safety:** Ensuring the safety of autonomous systems and their interactions with humans and the environment is paramount. Safety-critical applications such as autonomous vehicles must prioritize safety in decision making, incorporating fail-safe mechanisms and risk mitigation strategies to prevent accidents and minimize harm.

- **Ethical Dilemmas:** Autonomous systems may encounter ethical dilemmas when faced with conflicting objectives or values. For example, self-driving cars may need to make split-second decisions in life-threatening situations, such as choosing between colliding with pedestrians or swerving into oncoming traffic. Resolving ethical dilemmas requires ethical frameworks and decision-making algorithms that prioritize human welfare and adhere to moral principles.

4. Ethical Implications of Autonomous Decision Making

The ethical implications of autonomous decision making are far-reaching and multifaceted:

- **Accountability:** Determining accountability for the actions of autonomous systems poses a significant ethical challenge. Unlike humans, who can be held accountable for their decisions and actions, autonomous systems lack moral agency and cannot be held morally responsible for their behaviour Establishing mechanisms for attributing accountability and liability in cases of autonomous system failure or harm is essential for ensuring accountability and promoting trust in these technologies.

- **Bias and Fairness:** Autonomous systems may exhibit biases in decision making, reflecting biases present in the data used to train them or the algorithms themselves. Biased decisions can lead to unfair outcomes, perpetuating inequalities and discrimination. Addressing bias and promoting fairness in autonomous decision making requires proactive measures to detect, mitigate, and prevent biases throughout the AI lifecycle.

- **Transparency and Explainability:** Ensuring transparency and explainability in autonomous decision making is crucial for promoting trust, accountability, and user acceptance. Users must be able to understand how autonomous systems make decisions and why specific actions are chosen. Transparent decision-making processes enable users to validate and interpret the system's behavior, fostering trust and confidence in these technologies.

5. Future Directions and Considerations

As autonomous systems continue to evolve and proliferate, it is essential to address the ethical implications of their decision-making processes. Future research and development efforts should focus on:

- **Ethical Frameworks:** Developing ethical frameworks and guidelines for autonomous decision making that prioritize human welfare, fairness, and accountability.

- **Regulatory Oversight**: Establishing regulatory frameworks and oversight mechanisms to ensure ethical compliance and accountability in the design, deployment, and use of autonomous systems.

- **Public Engagement:** Engaging stakeholders, including policymakers, industry leaders, and the public, in discussions about the ethical implications of autonomous decision making and soliciting input on ethical guidelines and best practices.

Understanding autonomous systems' decision making is crucial for addressing the ethical implications of their actions. By prioritizing safety, fairness, transparency, and accountability in autonomous decision making, we can harness the potential of these technologies while minimizing risks and ensuring that they align with societal values and ethical principles.

Moral Agency in AI and Autonomous Agents

In the rapidly evolving landscape of artificial intelligence (AI) and autonomous agents, questions about moral agency and responsibility have become increasingly pertinent. As AI systems and autonomous agents gain greater autonomy and decision-making capabilities, there is a growing need to understand their capacity for moral agency and the ethical implications of their actions. This chapter explores the concept of moral agency in AI and autonomous agents, delving into the challenges, opportunities, and ethical considerations surrounding their role in moral decision-making.

1. Understanding Moral Agency

Moral agency refers to the capacity of an entity to act in accordance with moral principles and to be held accountable for its actions. Traditionally, moral agency has been attributed to humans who possess consciousness, intentionality, and the ability to reason about right and wrong. However, as AI systems and autonomous agents become increasingly sophisticated, questions arise about whether they can be considered moral agents in their own right.

2. AI Systems and Autonomous Agents: A Brief Overview

AI systems and autonomous agents encompass a broad spectrum of technologies, including robots, self-driving cars, virtual assistants, and chatbots. These systems are designed to perceive their environment, make decisions, and take actions autonomously, often based on complex algorithms and machine learning models. While AI systems lack consciousness and subjective experiences, they exhibit behaviors that mimic aspects of human intelligence, raising questions about their capacity for moral agency.

3. Challenges in Attributing Moral Agency to AI

Attributing moral agency to AI systems and autonomous agents presents several challenges:

- **Lack of Consciousness:** Unlike humans who possess subjective experiences and consciousness, AI systems lack subjective awareness and understanding of moral concepts. They operate based on algorithms and data-driven decision-making processes, without the capacity for introspection or moral reasoning.

- **Limited Autonomy:** While AI systems exhibit autonomy in performing tasks and making decisions within predefined parameters, their autonomy is constrained by their programming and design. They lack the capacity for free will or self-determination, which are essential attributes of moral agency.

- **Programming Biases:** AI systems may exhibit biases inherited from their training data or algorithmic design, leading to unfair or discriminatory outcomes. These biases can undermine their capacity for impartial moral decision-making and raise concerns about their ethical reliability.

4. Opportunities for Moral Decision-Making in AI

Despite these challenges, there are opportunities for integrating moral decision-making capabilities into AI systems and autonomous agents:

- **Ethical Design Principles:** Incorporating ethical design principles into the development of AI systems can promote ethical decision-making. Designing AI systems with transparency, fairness, and accountability in mind can help mitigate biases and ensure that their decisions align with moral principles.

- **Value Alignment:** Aligning the goals and objectives of AI systems with human values and ethical norms can guide their decision-making processes. By encoding ethical principles into their objectives and reward functions, AI systems can prioritize morally desirable outcomes in their actions.

- **Human Oversight and Control:** Providing mechanisms for human oversight and intervention in AI decision-making processes can enhance accountability and ethical governance. Human-in-the-loop systems enable humans to monitor, evaluate, and override AI decisions when necessary, ensuring alignment with moral principles.

5. Ethical Considerations and Implications

Addressing the ethical considerations and implications of moral agency in AI and autonomous agents is essential:

- **Accountability and Liability**: Determining accountability and liability for the actions of AI systems raises complex legal and ethical questions. Establishing frameworks for attributing responsibility and accountability in cases of AI failure or harm is crucial for ensuring legal and ethical compliance.

- **Transparency and Explainability:** Promoting transparency and explainability in AI decision-making processes is essential for fostering trust and accountability. Users must be able to understand how AI systems make decisions and why specific actions are chosen, enabling them to assess the ethical implications of AI-driven actions.

- **Ethical Oversight and Regulation:** Developing ethical oversight mechanisms and regulatory frameworks for AI systems can help ensure that they adhere to ethical standards and societal values. Ethical review boards, regulatory agencies, and industry standards bodies play a critical role in establishing guidelines and regulations for ethical AI development and deployment.

6. **Future Directions and Considerations**

As AI systems and autonomous agents continue to advance, several considerations warrant further exploration:

- **Ethical Education and Training:** Providing ethical education and training to AI developers, designers, and users can promote ethical awareness and responsible AI use. Incorporating ethics into STEM education and professional training programs can equip individuals with the knowledge and skills to navigate ethical challenges in AI development and deployment.

- **Ethical Governance and Oversight:** Strengthening ethical governance mechanisms and oversight structures for AI systems is essential for ensuring ethical compliance and accountability. Collaborative efforts among policymakers, industry leaders, researchers, and ethicists can inform the development of ethical guidelines, regulations, and standards for AI systems.

- **Interdisciplinary Research:** Facilitating interdisciplinary research and collaboration across fields such as ethics, computer science, law, and philosophy can enrich our understanding of moral agency in AI and autonomous agents. Integrating diverse perspectives and expertise can lead to more robust ethical frameworks and approaches for addressing moral challenges in AI development and deployment.

The concept of moral agency in AI and autonomous agents presents complex ethical challenges and opportunities. While AI systems lack consciousness and subjective experiences, they exhibit behaviors that raise questions about their capacity for moral decision-making. Addressing these challenges requires interdisciplinary collaboration, ethical governance, and transparency in AI development and deployment. By fostering ethical awareness, promoting value alignment, and prioritizing human oversight, we can navigate the ethical complexities of moral agency in AI and ensure that AI systems contribute to positive outcomes for society.

Assigning Moral Responsibility in Autonomous Systems

The advent of autonomous systems, powered by Artificial Intelligence (AI) and advanced robotics, poses profound questions about the assignment of moral responsibility. As these systems gain increasing autonomy and decision-making capabilities, determining who bears responsibility for their actions becomes a complex ethical challenge. In this chapter, we delve into the intricate landscape of assigning moral responsibility in autonomous systems, exploring the factors, dilemmas, and ethical considerations that shape this process.

1. Understanding Moral Responsibility

Moral responsibility refers to the accountability of individuals or entities for their actions, decisions, and their consequences in moral contexts. Traditionally, moral responsibility has been attributed to agents with consciousness, intentionality, and the capacity for rational deliberation. However, the emergence of autonomous systems complicates this traditional understanding, prompting revaluation of the criteria for moral responsibility in non-human entities.

2. The Rise of Autonomous Systems

Autonomous systems encompass a wide range of technologies, including self-driving cars, drones, and robotic assistants, designed to perform tasks and make decisions with varying degrees of independence. These systems operate based on algorithms, sensors, and machine learning models, enabling them to perceive their environment, process information, and act autonomously. As they become increasingly integrated into society, questions arise about how to attribute moral responsibility for their actions.

3. Challenges in Assigning Moral Responsibility

Assigning moral responsibility in autonomous systems presents several challenges:

- **Lack of Consciousness:** Autonomous systems lack consciousness and subjective experiences, raising questions about their capacity for moral agency. Unlike humans who possess self-awareness and moral reasoning abilities, autonomous systems operate based on preprogrammed algorithms and data-driven decision-making processes, without the ability to comprehend moral concepts.

- **Limited Autonomy:** While autonomous systems exhibit autonomy in performing tasks and making decisions within predefined parameters, their autonomy is constrained by their programming and design. They lack the capacity for intentionality or free will, essential attributes of moral agency, making it challenging to attribute moral responsibility to them for their actions.

- **Algorithmic Bias:** Autonomous systems may exhibit biases inherited from their training data or algorithmic design, leading to unfair or discriminatory outcomes. These biases can influence their decision-making processes and actions, raising questions about the ethical implications of their behavior and the assignment of moral responsibility.

4. Factors Influencing Moral Responsibility

Several factors influence the assignment of moral responsibility in autonomous systems:

- **Design and Programming:** The design and programming of autonomous systems play a significant role in shaping their behavior and decision-making processes. Ethical considerations must be integrated into the design phase to ensure that autonomous systems prioritize morally desirable outcomes and adhere to ethical principles.

- **Human Oversight and Control:** Human oversight and control mechanisms enable humans to monitor, evaluate, and intervene in the actions of autonomous systems. Human-in-the-loop systems allow humans to override autonomous decisions when necessary, mitigating the risk of unintended consequences and ensuring alignment with moral values.

- **Regulatory Frameworks:** Regulatory frameworks and legal standards play a crucial role in determining the allocation of moral responsibility in autonomous systems. Clear guidelines and regulations are needed to establish accountability and liability for the actions of autonomous systems, protecting individuals' rights and interests in cases of harm or wrongdoing.

5. Ethical Considerations in Assigning Moral Responsibility

Addressing the ethical considerations in assigning moral responsibility in autonomous systems is essential:

- **Accountability and Liability:** Determining accountability and liability for the actions of autonomous systems raises complex legal and ethical questions. Clear guidelines are needed to establish responsibility and ensure that appropriate measures are taken to address harm or wrongdoing caused by autonomous systems.

- **Transparency and Explainability:** Promoting transparency and explainability in the decision-making processes of autonomous systems is crucial for fostering trust and accountability. Users must be able to understand how autonomous systems make decisions and why specific actions are chosen, enabling them to assess the ethical implications of autonomous actions.

- **Fairness and Bias Mitigation:** Addressing biases and promoting fairness in the behavior of autonomous systems is essential for ensuring equitable outcomes. Measures such as bias detection, algorithmic auditing, and fairness-aware AI algorithms help identify and mitigate biases, promoting fairness and equity in autonomous decision-making.

6. Future Directions and Considerations

As autonomous systems continue to advance, several considerations warrant further exploration:

- **Ethical Education and Training:** Providing ethical education and training to developers, designers, and users of autonomous systems can promote ethical awareness and responsible behavior. Ethical considerations should be integrated into STEM education and professional training programs to equip individuals with the knowledge and skills to navigate ethical challenges in autonomous systems.

- **Ethical Governance and Oversight:** Strengthening ethical governance mechanisms and oversight structures for autonomous systems is essential for ensuring ethical compliance and accountability. Collaborative efforts among policymakers, industry leaders, researchers, and ethicists can inform the development of ethical guidelines, regulations, and standards for autonomous systems.

Assigning moral responsibility in autonomous systems is a complex and multifaceted endeavor that requires careful consideration of ethical principles, legal standards, and societal values. By integrating ethical considerations into the design, deployment, and governance of autonomous systems, we can navigate the ethical complexities of assigning moral responsibility and ensure that autonomous systems contribute to positive outcomes for society while upholding ethical standards and values. Through collaborative efforts and interdisciplinary dialogue, stakeholders can address the ethical challenges posed by autonomous systems and promote responsible behavior in the development and use of these technologies.

Chapter 10
Ethical Challenges in Autonomous Vehicles

The emergence of autonomous vehicles heralds a transformative era in transportation, promising enhanced safety, efficiency, and mobility. However, alongside their potential benefits, autonomous vehicles present a myriad of ethical challenges that demand careful consideration and resolution. This chapter explores the ethical complexities surrounding autonomous vehicles, delving into dilemmas such as decision-making in moral dilemmas, liability and accountability, and societal impacts. As autonomous vehicles navigate the roads, they must grapple with moral dilemmas previously reserved for human drivers, raising questions about the prioritization of passenger safety, pedestrian welfare, and ethical decision-making algorithms. Moreover, issues of liability and accountability loom large, as the responsibility for accidents and errors shifts from human drivers to vehicle manufacturers, programmers, and regulatory bodies. Additionally, the widespread adoption of autonomous vehicles has far-reaching societal implications, including effects on employment, urban planning, and environmental sustainability. By confronting these ethical challenges head-on, stakeholders can pave the way for the responsible development and deployment of autonomous vehicles that prioritize safety, fairness, and the greater societal good.

Ethical Dilemmas Faced by Autonomous Vehicles

Autonomous vehicles represent a paradigm shift in transportation, promising safer, more efficient, and convenient mobility. However, the adoption of autonomous driving technology also introduces a host of ethical dilemmas that challenge traditional notions of morality and decision-making. In this chapter, we delve into the ethical dilemmas faced by autonomous vehicles, exploring the complexities of navigating moral decisions on the road.

1. Moral Decision-Making in Autonomous Vehicles

Autonomous vehicles rely on complex algorithms and sensors to perceive their surroundings and make split-second decisions while driving. These decisions often involve navigating moral dilemmas where the vehicle must choose between potentially harmful outcomes. For example, in a situation where a collision is unavoidable, should the vehicle prioritize the safety of its occupants, or should it prioritize avoiding harm to pedestrians or other road users?

2. The Trolley Problem and Variants

The classic trolley problem serves as a theoretical framework for understanding moral decision-making in autonomous vehicles. In its simplest form, the trolley problem presents a scenario where a runaway trolley is on course to collide with multiple people, and the decision-maker must choose whether to divert the trolley onto a track where it will harm fewer people. Similarly, autonomous vehicles may face analogous situations where they must choose between different courses of action, each with potentially harmful consequences.

3. Prioritization of Occupant Safety vs. Pedestrian Welfare

One of the most pressing ethical dilemmas faced by autonomous vehicles involves the prioritization of occupant safety versus pedestrian welfare. Should autonomous vehicles prioritize protecting their occupants at all costs, even if it means putting pedestrians at risk? Conversely, should they prioritize minimizing harm to pedestrians, potentially endangering the occupants of the vehicle?

4. Risk Management and Uncertainty

Autonomous vehicles must also contend with uncertainty and imperfect information when making decisions on the road. Factors such as unpredictable human behavior, adverse weather conditions, and mechanical failures introduce variability and risk into driving scenarios. Balancing the need to make timely decisions with the inherent uncertainty of the environment presents a significant challenge for autonomous vehicles.

5. Legal and Regulatory Considerations

The ethical dilemmas faced by autonomous vehicles raise complex legal and regulatory questions. Who should be held liable in the event of an accident involving an autonomous vehicle? Should manufacturers, programmers, or regulatory bodies bear responsibility for the vehicle's actions? Developing clear guidelines and regulations that govern the behavior of autonomous vehicles while also addressing ethical concerns is crucial for ensuring accountability and safety on the roads.

6. Societal Impacts and Equity

The widespread adoption of autonomous vehicles has far-reaching societal implications beyond individual decision-making dilemmas. Autonomous vehicles have the potential to reshape urban landscapes, alter transportation patterns, and impact employment in industries such as transportation and logistics. Ensuring equitable access to autonomous transportation and addressing potential disparities in its deployment are important considerations for policymakers and stakeholders.

7. Ethical Design and Transparency

Addressing the ethical dilemmas faced by autonomous vehicles requires a multifaceted approach that prioritizes ethical design, transparency, and stakeholder engagement. Designing ethical decision-making algorithms that prioritize human safety and well-being while also considering societal values and preferences is essential. Additionally, ensuring transparency in how autonomous vehicles make decisions and communicate with other road users fosters trust and acceptance of this emerging technology.

The ethical dilemmas faced by autonomous vehicles underscore the complex intersection of technology, morality, and society. By grappling with these challenges and developing ethical frameworks that guide the behavior of autonomous vehicles, we can harness the potential of this technology to improve road safety, enhance mobility, and contribute to the greater societal good. Through interdisciplinary collaboration, stakeholder engagement, and ongoing dialogue, we can navigate the ethical complexities of autonomous driving and pave the way for a future where autonomous vehicles coexist responsibly with humans on the roads.

Approaches to Solving Moral Decision Making in Autonomous Vehicle

As autonomous vehicles (AVs) become increasingly prevalent on our roads, the ethical dilemmas they face in decision-making become more pronounced. To address these challenges, various approaches have been proposed to guide the moral decision-making processes of AVs. In this chapter, we explore these approaches in detail, focusing on their strengths, limitations, and implications for the future of autonomous driving.

1. Utilitarianism-Based Approaches

Utilitarianism, a moral theory that advocates maximizing overall happiness or utility, has been proposed as a guiding principle for AV decision-making. Under this approach, AVs prioritize outcomes that result in the least harm or maximize overall welfare, regardless of individual interests. For example, in a scenario where a collision is imminent, AVs programmed with utilitarian principles would prioritize minimizing the total number of casualties, even if it means sacrificing the safety of the vehicle's occupants.

Strengths:

- Utilitarian-based approaches offer a clear and objective criterion for decision-making, focusing on maximizing overall societal welfare.
- Prioritizing the greater good aligns with ethical principles that prioritize minimizing harm and promoting well-being.

Limitations:

- Utilitarian approaches may sacrifice individual rights and interests in favor of the collective good, raising concerns about fairness and justice.
- Implementing utilitarian principles in AV decision-making requires quantifying and comparing different outcomes, which may be challenging in practice.

2. Deontological Approaches

Deontological ethics, which emphasizes adherence to moral principles or duties, offers an alternative framework for guiding AV decision-making. Under this approach, AVs are programmed to follow predefined rules or principles, regardless of the consequences. For example, AVs may be programmed to prioritize avoiding harm to innocent bystanders, even if it means sacrificing the safety of the vehicle's occupants.

Strengths:

- Deontological approaches prioritize respect for moral principles and rights, promoting consistency and predictability in decision-making.
- By adhering to predefined rules, deontological AVs may provide a sense of reassurance and trust to users and stakeholders.

Limitations:

- Deontological approaches may be rigid and inflexible, leading to situations where adherence to rules results in suboptimal outcomes.
- Determining the appropriate set of rules or principles for AV decision-making may be challenging and subject to debate.

3. Virtue Ethics-Based Approaches

Virtue ethics, which focuses on the character and moral virtues of individuals, offers another perspective on AV decision-making. Under this approach, AVs are programmed to exhibit virtuous traits such as empathy, compassion, and responsibility in their interactions with others. For example, AVs may prioritize actions that demonstrate care for all stakeholders and foster trust and cooperation on the roads.

Strengths:

- Virtue ethics-based approaches emphasize the importance of character and integrity in decision-making, promoting ethical behavior and trustworthiness.

- By embodying virtuous traits, AVs may contribute to a more harmonious and cooperative environment on the roads.

Limitations:

- Virtue ethics-based approaches may be subjective and culturally contingent, leading to variations in moral judgments across different contexts.
- Implementing virtue ethics in AV decision-making requires defining and operationalizing virtuous traits in a way that is applicable to autonomous systems.

4. Hybrid and Adaptive Approaches

Recognizing the limitations of individual ethical theories, some researchers advocate for hybrid or adaptive approaches that integrate multiple ethical principles into AV decision-making. These approaches aim to balance competing moral considerations and adapt to different contexts and preferences. For example, AVs may employ a combination of utilitarian, deontological, and virtue ethics-based principles depending on the specific circumstances.

Strengths:

- Hybrid and adaptive approaches offer flexibility and adaptability in decision-making, allowing AVs to respond to a wide range of situations and preferences.
- By integrating multiple ethical principles, these approaches may provide a more nuanced and contextually sensitive approach to AV decision-making.

Limitations:

- Implementing hybrid and adaptive approaches requires sophisticated decision-making algorithms and systems that can integrate and prioritize different ethical principles in real-time.

- Balancing competing ethical considerations and preferences may be challenging and require trade-offs that are difficult to reconcile.

5. Stakeholder Engagement and Ethical Deliberation

In addition to algorithmic approaches, some scholars emphasize the importance of stakeholder engagement and ethical deliberation in shaping AV decision-making. By involving diverse stakeholders, including policymakers, ethicists, engineers, and the public, in discussions about ethical priorities and trade-offs, AV developers can foster transparency, accountability, and trust in the technology.

Strengths:

- Stakeholder engagement and ethical deliberation promote transparency and inclusivity in decision-making, ensuring that a wide range of perspectives and values are considered.
- By involving stakeholders in the decision-making process, AV developers can build consensus around ethical priorities and foster public acceptance of autonomous driving technology.

Limitations:

- Stakeholder engagement and ethical deliberation may be time-consuming and resource-intensive, requiring careful facilitation and coordination.
- Balancing the interests and preferences of diverse stakeholders may be challenging, leading to conflicts and disagreements about ethical priorities and trade-offs.

The ethical dilemmas faced by autonomous vehicles require careful consideration and deliberation to develop responsible and ethically sound solutions. By exploring and integrating different ethical approaches, engaging stakeholders in ethical deliberation, and prioritizing transparency and accountability, we can navigate the complexities of AV decision-making and ensure that autonomous vehicles contribute to safer, more ethical transportation systems. Through interdisciplinary collaboration, ongoing dialogue, and ethical reflection, we can pave the way for a future where autonomous vehicles prioritize human welfare, fairness, and the greater societal good.

Public Perception and Acceptance of Ethical AI in Transportation

The integration of Artificial Intelligence (AI) into transportation systems promises significant advancements in safety, efficiency, and sustainability. However, alongside these benefits, the ethical implications of AI in transportation have garnered increasing attention from the public and policymakers. Understanding public perception and acceptance of ethical AI in transportation is crucial for fostering trust, addressing concerns, and shaping the future development and deployment of AI-driven transportation technologies. In this chapter, we explore the nuances of public perception and acceptance of ethical AI in transportation, examining key factors, challenges, and opportunities for building a more ethically conscious transportation ecosystem.

1. Understanding Public Perception of Ethical AI in Transportation

Public perception of ethical AI in transportation is influenced by a myriad of factors, including trust in technology, concerns about safety and privacy, and perceptions of fairness and accountability. Surveys and studies have revealed a range of attitudes and opinions among the public regarding the ethical implications of AI in transportation, from cautious optimism to skepticism and apprehension. Factors such as previous experiences with AI technologies, media coverage of AI-related incidents, and cultural values shape individuals' perceptions and attitudes towards AI in transportation.

2. Factors Influencing Public Acceptance of Ethical AI in Transportation

Several factors play a significant role in shaping public acceptance of ethical AI in transportation:

- **Safety and Reliability:** Public trust in AI-driven transportation technologies is closely tied to perceptions of safety and reliability. Concerns about the potential for accidents, errors, and malfunctions in AI systems can undermine public confidence and acceptance.

- **Transparency and Explainability:** Transparency and explainability are essential for fostering public trust in AI systems. Individuals want assurance that AI-driven transportation systems are transparent about their decision-making processes, algorithms, and data usage, allowing users to understand and validate their behavior.

- **Privacy and Data Security:** Privacy concerns are a major consideration for the public when it comes to AI in transportation. Individuals are wary of potential surveillance, data breaches, and unauthorized access to personal information by AI systems, leading to apprehension and reluctance to adopt these technologies.

- **Equity and Accessibility:** Ensuring equity and accessibility in AI-driven transportation systems is critical for public acceptance. Concerns about disparities in access, affordability, and service quality can undermine confidence in these technologies, particularly among marginalized communities.

- **Ethical Considerations:** Public awareness and concern about ethical considerations such as fairness, bias, and accountability are growing. Individuals expect AI-driven transportation systems to adhere to ethical principles, prioritize safety, and mitigate risks of harm or discrimination.

3. **Challenges in Building Public Trust and Acceptance**

Despite the potential benefits of ethical AI in transportation, several challenges hinder efforts to build public trust and acceptance:

- **Perception of Risk:** Public perception of AI-driven transportation technologies is often influenced by perceptions of risk and uncertainty. High-profile incidents or accidents involving AI systems can amplify concerns and erode public confidence, even if the overall safety record of these technologies is favorable.

- **Lack of Understanding:** Many individuals have limited understanding of AI technologies and their implications in transportation. Misconceptions, misinformation, and lack of awareness contribute to skepticism and apprehension towards AI-driven transportation systems.

- **Ethical Concerns:** Ethical considerations such as bias, fairness, and accountability raise complex questions that challenge public acceptance. Addressing these concerns requires transparent communication, robust ethical frameworks, and mechanisms for accountability and oversight.

- **Regulatory and Policy Uncertainty:** Uncertainty surrounding regulations and policies governing AI in transportation can create confusion and hesitation among stakeholders. Clear guidelines and standards are needed to provide clarity and guidance for the development and deployment of AI-driven transportation technologies.

4. Opportunities for Building Public Trust and Acceptance

Despite these challenges, there are opportunities to enhance public trust and acceptance of ethical AI in transportation:

- **Transparency and Engagement:** Open communication and stakeholder engagement are essential for building trust and fostering public acceptance of AI-driven transportation technologies. Providing clear information about how AI systems work, their benefits, and potential risks can empower individuals to make informed decisions and participate in the development process.

- **Ethical Design and Accountability:** Prioritizing ethical design principles and accountability mechanisms can enhance public confidence in AI-driven transportation systems. Incorporating safeguards against bias, ensuring fairness and equity, and establishing mechanisms for redress and accountability can mitigate concerns and build trust.

- **Education and Awareness:** Increasing public awareness and understanding of AI technologies and their ethical implications is crucial. Education initiatives, public forums, and outreach efforts can empower individuals to engage in informed discussions about AI in transportation and contribute to shaping ethical practices and policies.

- **Demonstrating Benefits:** Highlighting the tangible benefits of AI-driven transportation, such as improved safety, efficiency, and accessibility, can build public confidence and acceptance. Real-world demonstrations, pilot projects, and case studies showcasing the positive impact of AI technologies can help overcome skepticism and resistance.

Public perception and acceptance of ethical AI in transportation play a pivotal role in shaping the trajectory of AI-driven transportation technologies. By addressing concerns, fostering trust, and prioritizing ethical principles, stakeholders can build a transportation ecosystem that harnesses the potential of AI to improve safety, efficiency, and accessibility while upholding societal values and priorities. Through collaborative efforts, transparent communication, and proactive engagement with the public, we can create a future where AI-driven transportation systems are embraced as safe, reliable, and ethically sound solutions for the challenges of the modern world.

www.ingramcontent.com/pod-product-compliance
Lightning Source LLC
LaVergne TN
LVHW061552070526
838199LV00077B/7007